FLAVORS OF THE SOUTHEAST ASIAN GRILL

FLAVORS OF THE
SOUTHEAST
ASIAN GRILL

Classic Recipes for Seafood and
Meats Cooked over Charcoal

LEELA PUNYARATABANDHU

Photographs by David Loftus

TEN SPEED PRESS
California | New York

FOR ISAAC

CONTENTS

RECIPE LIST

INTRODUCTION

I'd thought about starting this book with something lyrical—maybe a harkening back to our collective past as humans first discovering and then cooking with fire. Next I'd cite a poetic quote from a scientist or an archaeologist about how we are bound together regardless of race through our love of the scent of smoke, which I'd follow with how I was inspired by the daily aroma of food grilling on a clay charcoal stove when I was growing up in Thailand. But I decided against that beginning. You see, the impetus for this book is much more practical than it is romantic.

It started with—let me set the scene—me eating at a stateside Thai restaurant many years ago. As I examined a skewer of chicken satay in my hand, I knew it had been cooked on a griddle hours in advance and reheated in a microwave, which prompted me to let out a small sigh over the wretched fate of how such an iconic grilled dish had become so dry, bland, and utterly devoid of smokiness. Anyone, I thought, could make this so much better at home.

Grilled dishes are among the most glorious creations of Southeast Asian cuisines, but they're rarely on Asian restaurant menus in the West. And the ones that are served, such as satay, are nearly always translated poorly, leaving few traces of their original glories. I've discovered that when Southeast Asian grilling is mentioned, the response is too often a blank stare. Most people think first of the East Asian traditions of Korean indoor tabletop barbecue and the bite-size grilled morsels served in a Japanese *izakaya*. Both lend themselves better to indoor dining, and because people in the West primarily experience global cuisines through their local restaurants, they are better known than their Southeast Asian outdoor counterparts.

You can't blame anyone. In Southeast Asia, people often enjoy grilled food in open-air markets, rather than in sit-down, enclosed food venues. Remove the cooking over charcoal and wood from that culinary culture and a big chasm opens up. Unfortunately, live-fire cooking—a prominent, glorious feature of the Southeast Asian food scene—is not practical in American restaurants, which are governed by rigorous safety codes and regulations. What we end up with is satay seared on a griddle—a result miles away from skewered meat charred over a live fire, where it absorbs a heady mix of aromatic herbs and spices and of fat dripping onto sizzling, hissing, smoking hot coals.

But the blessings are, as is often said, hidden in plain sight. It's also in the West, especially in the United States, where you find a strong DIY mentality, a large collective body of grilling and barbecuing knowledge and technology, and the abundant availability of grilling and smoking tools for home use, all of which more than make up for a scarcity of open-air night markets and street-food culture. The vibrant, widespread culture of tailgate parties, backyard cookouts, summer picnics, home-built smokehouses, and more makes it all even better.

The best place outside Southeast Asia to experience the region's grilled and smoked dishes as they're meant to be enjoyed is not, in fact, at an Asian restaurant. It's in your own backyard.

ABOUT THIS BOOK

Flavors of the Southeast Asian Grill is by no means an exhaustive compendium of the iconic grilled and smoked dishes of Southeast Asia, with every country represented equally. Nor is it a cultural, culinary, or anthropological survey of the region.

Instead, it is a collection of my favorite dishes from my childhood in Thailand and from traveling, eating, and cooking widely throughout Southeast Asia as an adult. A number of the recipes come from my family's collections, and others are from friends who live in the region. Many more are the result of my obsessions both with re-creating the dishes that I've enjoyed and with perfecting new cooking techniques I've picked up during my years of writing about food.

However, my personal connection with a dish wasn't the only criterion I used to determine what to include out of my vast collection of favorites. One very important consideration was how practical it would be to replicate the recipes in a typical Western home. All of them, therefore, are relatively simple to prepare, though some require more steps than others and are more suitable for a weekend project. Plus, they can all be made with the tools that grilling and barbecuing enthusiasts already have or can acquire easily.

I have also considered the availability of ingredients and have left out dishes – regardless of how iconic – that call for key items found only in Asia. The recipes that follow are the ones that I routinely make in the backyard of my home in Chicagoland and for which I can find either the traditional ingredients or acceptable substitutes.

Finally, though I have remained true to the flavors and presentations of these dishes as I have experienced them in their home regions, I use cuts of meat that are widely sold in North America. Each region has its own way of butchering animals, its own preferred animal parts, and its own traditions for cutting them up for cooking. You're not going to find, for example, St. Louis–style pork ribs at any market in Laos, unless you know a butcher and show him exactly how you want your spareribs trimmed. Likewise, many cuts of meat commonly used in certain dishes in Southeast Asia are not easily found in other parts of the world. Culinary purists' eyebrows will raise, as they are wont to do, but rigid insistence on using only those cuts when others that are easy to find will work just as well is foolhardy and doesn't benefit anyone.

EQUIPMENT, TOOLS & FUELS

Home-style grilling and smoking in Southeast Asia are usually done very simply. The traditional clay charcoal grill, which is modestly built and often portable, covers everyday grilling needs, as does the hibachi-style grill. Walk around a rural market anywhere in the region and you'll come across all sorts of live-fire contraptions put together—out of creativity and necessity—from things that were never meant to be used for grilling. Anything that can withstand high heat can be used, it seems.

Smoking requires a more elaborate setup, but it's still done in a rustic and simple manner at home. People tend to leave anything complex, such as roasting a suckling pig or smoking fish on a large scale, to food vendors, artisans, and caterers.

When I arrived in Chicago to attend school several years ago, I was well versed in using the traditional Thai clay grill. But when I tried to cook on a small American-style kettle grill, I had to relearn everything I thought I knew, from how to start a fire to how to control the heat to how to achieve maximum fuel efficiency. Once I became acclimated to Western-style grilling and smoking tools, however, I realized that even though they were different and required different skills, they worked well for cooking all of my favorite grilled and smoked dishes from home. I will always love the traditional grills, but I don't really need them, and neither do you.

For the purpose of making the recipes in this book, I recommend the following tools.

Grills & Other Outdoor Cookers

KETTLE GRILL

This basic yet reliable tool is what most people have at home, and for a good reason: it's affordable, easy to find, easy to use, and easy to move around. You can even turn it into a smoker, which makes it ideal for people with limited space or for those who don't want to buy another piece of equipment when they just want to smoke something once in a while. A kettle grill comes with two vents: a bottom vent, called the intake damper, and a top vent, called the exhaust damper. You use both to control the temperature of the grill. Depending on the type and brand of your grill, the vents can be adjusted through various settings, so consult your grill manual. Weber (weber.com) makes the kettle grill in several models and sizes, all of which are reliable and perform well.

To turn a kettle grill into a smoker, you'll need some wood chips and a heavy-duty disposable foil pan large enough to cover half of the bottom of the grill. Start by soaking your smoking wood chips in water for at least 2 hours or up to overnight and then drain them. Fill the foil pan half full with water and put the pan to one side of the grill bottom. Light a full chimney starter (see page 7) of charcoal, and when the coals are ready, pour them out onto the empty side of the grill bottom. When the coals are covered with white ash, spread the moist wood chips over them. Position the grate on the grill and put the food you'd like to smoke on the grate directly above the water pan. Cover the grill and close the vents. Using a grill thermometer (see page 7), monitor the temperature closely. To keep the temperature in the range specified in the recipe, adjust the vents to increase or decrease the airflow: open the vents for greater flow and a hotter fire; narrow the vents for less flow and a cooler fire. If the temperature drops too low to revive it to the target temperature, you will need to add more hot coals and soaked wood chips.

VERTICAL WATER SMOKER

Shaped like a spaceship, the vertical water smoker is affordable, offers the flexibility of a grill and smoker combo, and doesn't take a lot of space. For smoking, it employs a water pan, which is placed in the middle section between the coals and the cooking grate to provide moisture to the smoking chamber and help maintain an ideal smoking temperature (225° to 250°F). Just as a kettle grill can be rigged into a smoker, a

vertical water smoker can be used as a grill, albeit a small one. All you need to do is remove the middle section and you instantly have a short-legged kettle grill. That makes it another great choice for people who don't have room for both a smoker and a grill. The Weber Smoky Mountain (weber.com) is the most popular vertical water smoker.

KAMADO

This egg-shaped ceramic grill is essentially the modern version of an ancient Japanese earthenware cooking vessel. It is a grill, smoker, and oven in one very heavy piece of equipment. Its thick, dense ceramic wall is great at absorbing and maintaining heat and in keeping smoke inside, which also means lower charcoal consumption. Although you will need to control the temperature manually by adjusting the dampers, the kamado doesn't need a lot of babysitting. It is a wonderful stand-in for the clay jar oven (see page 66) or smoker used in some parts of Southeast Asia (follow the manufacturer's instructions for how to set up a kamado grill for smoking). A ceramic grill is quite expensive, but with proper care, it lasts a lifetime.

The Big Green Egg (biggreenegg.com) is the pioneering brand on the market and by far the most popular. Other brands and models are available, however. The Slow 'N Sear Deluxe Kamado (abcbarbecue.com), for example, makes it easy to create a two-zone cooking surface, which has often been a challenge in a kamado.

HIBACHI

This type of grill is small and uncomplicated, which is why it is loved for its portability and ease of use. A hibachi isn't as versatile as other grills, but it's perfect for making satay or any recipe in this book that involves quick cooking and searing of meat on short skewers over a direct fire. This is because the handles of the skewers extend outside the small, hot cooking area. As a result, they remain cool enough to handle and, in the case of bamboo skewers, are not at risk of burning. You'll find several inexpensive hibachi grills to choose from, but my favorite is the cast-iron Sportman's Grill made by Lodge (lodgemfg.com).

BARREL COOKER

Also known as an ugly drum smoker, a barrel cooker is a charcoal smoker made out of a thirty- to fifty-five-gallon steel drum. A basket of lit charcoal is placed at the bottom of the barrel, and the meat is hung from the top. When cooked in a cylindrical cooker like this, the meat is heated from all sides at once (the heat stays steady at 275° to 315°F), resulting in evenly cooked, succulent meat. The fat, protein, and seasonings in the marinade drop down to the coals below and produce a delicious smoky flavor that perfumes the meat. One of my favorite pieces of equipment for cooking meat, this affordable smoker is easy to set up and reliable and doesn't need to be constantly monitored. When chicken is cooked in a barrel cooker, it comes out very juicy, even the breasts. My favorite brand is Pit Barrel Cooker (pitbarrelcooker.com).

PELLET GRILL/SMOKER

This grill and smoker combo requires electricity, but that's what makes it easy to use. A pellet grill uses an auger to move hardwood pellets from the hopper to the fire pot inside the grill. Once the pellets hit the fire pot, they get ignited. A fan then stokes the fire, creating an environment similar to a convection oven but with smoke. With a pellet grill, you can set a temperature, put the food in, and forget it. Even people who have never smoked anything find smoking with a pellet grill easy.

PIG ROASTING BOX

Designed primarily for roasting a whole pig, this metal-lined wooden box works like an oven, with the heat source of burning coals spread on the lid. A pig roasting box is big and takes up quite a bit of space, but you can also use it the same way you would an oven to cook several smaller pieces of meat at the same time. Also, while the coals on the lid are cooking the pig in the chamber below, you can place a cooking rack over the coals and grill all sorts of other things. La Caja China (lacajachina.com) makes good ones.

Grilling Tools

The usual grilling accessories that you can find where grills and smokers are sold will come in handy for making the recipes in this book. You don't need everything a clerk tries to sell you, however. Here are a few necessities.

THERMOMETER

When it comes to temperature, the ability to be precise is good, but for the purposes of this book, common-sense is more important than having a state-of-the-art thermometer. A charcoal grill is not like an oven where you set it at the desired temperature and it stays there. When it comes to cooking over live fire, it's more important to develop observation skills to figure out the hot and cold spots on your grill, to notice the rate at which your food is cooking, and to know when and how to slow it down or speed it up, among other things.

That being said, in some cases, especially when you're smoking, it's important to be precise. Having a reliable grill thermometer is, therefore, helpful. A built-in thermometer on the grill lid isn't reliable, and the hand test, in which you gauge the temperature by how many seconds you can hold your palm over the fire before pulling it away, doesn't work well in every situation. Use your thermometer to help build high heat (500° to 650°F), medium-high heat (400° to 450°F), medium heat (350° to 375°F), and medium-low heat (300° to 325°F).

In addition to a thermometer for the grill and smoker, you'll also need a thermometer for your food because visual cues alone aren't always enough to guide you when it comes to grilling and smoking. I recommend the wireless remote digital thermometer with dual probe that is left in the food during cooking. It will give you real-time temperatures of both the grill or smoker and the food.

CHIMNEY STARTER

In Thailand, people start a clay charcoal stove or grill with *tai*, the traditional fire starter made from sawdust that is bound together with tree resin or oil, and they stoke the fire with a woven bamboo fan. In the United States, I prefer a chimney starter and small paraffin cubes (both made by Weber) to start my fire. That combination is a quick, foolproof method. It typically takes from 10 to 15 minutes from the charcoal in a chimney starter to go from cold briquettes to glowing coals partially covered with ash—ready for pouring into the grill, where they will be arranged into a two-zone fire (see page 11) or for direct-heat cooking (see page 14).

HEAT-RESISTANT GLOVES

If you plan to cook with a kamado, a barrel cooker, or a pig roasting box, a pair of good-quality, heat-resistant gloves is necessary. Buy the longest ones you can find to ensure your arms are protected. You can get away without these gloves when cooking with the basic kettle grill, but I always find them useful in all grilling situation even when I cook on a small hibachi grill.

GRILLING TONGS

I can't imagine grilling without my heavy-duty tongs. I have at least two pairs near me at all times. I use one to take the coals out of the bag, to move the coals around the grill, to shake the ash off the coals, and sometimes to adjust the grill grate. I use the other to transfer food to and from the grill and to flip, roll, and move it as it's cooked. The tongs need to be sturdy without being too difficult to squeeze (as some cheap ones are). They should be stainless steel and 16 inches long, and they should come with a convenient locking mechanism. All things being equal, a pair of tongs that feels most natural in your hand—like an extension of it—will work best.

FUELS

If anything wedges a gap between the grilled and smoked dishes as made in Southeast Asia and the same dishes made in your backyard, it's not the equipment or the technique. Rather, it's the fuels, which is to be expected. In live-fire cooking, people from every culture use the native plants and trees around them for fuel. These natural products have, in turn, created the scent, color, and other characteristics that the locals associate with each dish—characteristics that are sometimes regarded as defining factors.

>> CONTINUED ON PAGE 11

One example is the Indonesian smoked meat *se'i*, which comes from Kupang, the capital of the province of East Nusa Tenggara. *Se'i* is essentially no different from the salt-cured meat found in other parts of Asia. But the meat is traditionally smoked with the leaves and wood from the kesambi or lac tree *Schleichera oleosa* (Lour) Oken, which is native to the Indian subcontinent and Southeast Asia and is what gives the meat its distinctive aroma and reddish color. You could replicate the dish using, say, pecan wood, but the result—which would be a delicious dish in its own right—would strip *se'i* of its uniqueness and render it nearly indistinguishable from similar types of smoked meat. For this reason, the recipes I've chosen for this book are far less dependent on native fuels.

That said, because of the dissimilarities in flora and climate, some minor differences will need to be accepted. In Southeast Asia, one of the most highly prized fuels for grilling and smoking is charcoal made from mangrove, a shrub or small tree that grows in coastal swamps throughout the region. Rambutan, guava, rubber, and other types of local woods are increasingly common these days as well. Bagasse, the desiccated pulp residue left after juice has been extracted from sugarcane, is another regularly used fuel. Dried corncobs stripped of kernels and the husks of mature coconuts are also favored. None of these fuels is easy to find outside the region.

Fortunately, you can make every recipe in this book successfully using the fuels that are affordable and widely available to you. Meathead Goldwyn, author of *Meathead: The Science of Great Barbecue and Grilling*, writes on his website, amazingribs.com, "A lot of cooks swear by one fuel or another with vehement conviction, but I'm here to tell you, it is all much ado about little. The quality of the raw food is far more important. The seasonings are far more important. And without a doubt, getting food off the heat at the right internal temperature is far more important." That sound you just heard is me, a bag of supermarket charcoal briquettes held aloft, shouting amen.

In an ideal world, you'll be able to smoke *sai ua* (page 155) with coconut husks, the typical fuel choice in Thailand. But in the United States, I'd take the hickory- or cherrywood-smoked version of this iconic sausage any day, given that even vendors in Thailand are often taking shortcuts and either deep-frying it or cooking it on an electric griddle, which are far worse than smoking the sausage with a wood that's not native to Asia. Likewise, mangrove charcoal is the sought-after fuel for grilling northeastern Thai–style grilled chicken, but when one considers the detrimental environmental issues stemming from mangrove deforestation in Southeast Asia, even the mangrove-wood-only crowd finds it can get used to cooking with other types of wood.

That means that the charcoal briquettes and lump charcoal that are widely available will work well for all of the recipes in this book. This also applies to wood chunks, chips, pellets, and blocks. As for which type of wood to use for smoking, I have made suggestions in the recipe headnotes.

The Two-Zone Grilling Method

In keeping with the simple, fuss-free theme, the only technique you need to master in order to make the recipes in this book is the two-zone method (see page 11). This involves setting up your grill so the coals are piled to one side, leaving the other side empty. That way, you can sear and char your food over direct radiant heat (the hot side) and slowly bring it to the desired internal temperature over indirect convection heat (the cooler side, aka the hold side). You can control the heat by moving food back and forth between the two zones as needed to prevent it from burning before it's cooked through. Adjusting the vents to regulate the amount of air going into the grill (the more air, the hotter the grill gets) is another way to control the heat.

To set up a two-zone grill, start by lighting a full chimney of charcoal. When the coals are glowing and partially dusted with ash, deposit them on one side of the grill.

The Direct-Heat Grilling Method

As versatile and useful as the two-zone grilling setup is, in some situations, the benefits of being able to maximize the grilling surface outweigh the benefits of having multiple grilling areas with different temperatures. In these cases, you spread lit coals all over the bottom of the grill as opposed to piling them to one side of it.

Thin slices or small pieces of meat, thin chops, and vegetables are some examples of things for which you don't really need the two-zone setup. A smaller grill, like a hibachi grill, is ideal for this "hot and fast" grilling.

HOW TO COMPOSE A MEAL THE SOUTHEAST ASIAN WAY

In the West, a protein-rich dish is the center of the meal, and everything else is served in smaller portions as sides. But in most of Asia, including Southeast Asia, the starch—nearly always rice—is the center of the meal. It is typically served with multiple dishes, which come to the table all at once—even soup and salad. Ideally these "rice accompaniments" work together to create a meal with a variety of complementary flavors, textures, colors, and even temperatures. Keep in mind, therefore, that most of the recipes in this book are seasoned amply to compensate for the blandness of the rice they've been created to accompany.

Observant people who have spent time in Southeast Asia will notice that even though people—in theory—can compose their meal in any way or with any components they want, certain patterns, repeated often enough and for long enough to have become well-established cultural norms, tend to dictate their choices. For example, northeastern Thai–style grilled chicken, cooked glutinous rice (aka sticky rice), and a spicy vegetable salad made with green papaya, cucumbers, or bamboo shoots make for a popular combination. Replacing the sticky rice in this meal with plain long-grain rice, fried rice, or coconut rice is, of course, permissible. But it would be as strange to the Thais as replacing the chips in fish and chips with, say, potato salad. Likewise, a satay meal in Singapore and Malaysia often comes with plain rice dumplings, which you could replace with sticky rice or steamed jasmine rice. But, again, it would seem as out of place to the locals as replacing cornbread with croissants in a down-home American barbecue meal.

When you cook and dine in your own home, however, you should not be bound by anything other than what you and your family or friends want to eat. So think of the recipes and suggested meals in this book as starting points based on tradition and feel free to make your own rules as you go along.

I have decided to focus on what you need to know and have in order to execute the recipes in this book successfully, rather than inundating you with information. But if you would like to know more about grilling and barbecuing, see the Recommended Reading List on page 203.

FISH & SHELLFISH

CEDAR-PLANK SALMON SALAD BITES

Called *miang* in Thailand, this fun appetizer lends itself to communal cooking and eating. On a weekend, family members come together to help cut various flavorful ingredients into little pieces so that later they can all sit down together and compose and consume bite-size salad wraps made up of the finely cut foods. *Miang* is also by definition flexible. Other than a few iterations that have become essentially canonized, it can contain anything you want. You are in charge of the destiny of your *miang*. Think of it as a salad that is composed on the palm of a hand, one bite at a time.

The grilling of the salmon on a cedar plank is the American influence. This way I can juxtapose the smoky result with the vibrant flavors of lime, chiles, and ginger—all against the backdrop of fragrant fresh herbs. And though there are other ways to introduce smokiness to the fish, the plank makes for a great presentation as well as eliminates any possibility of the fish sticking to the grate. You'll need a cedar plank, about 12 inches long.

SERVES 4 AS AN APPETIZER

Soak the cedar planks in warm water to cover for 1 hour.

To make the dressing: In a small food processor or a mortar, blend the chiles and garlic until the bits are the size of a match head. Transfer to a small saucepan, add the fish sauce and sugar, and heat gently over medium heat just until the sugar dissolves. Remove from the heat, stir in the lime juice, and transfer to a small heatproof serving bowl.

To cook the fish: Pat the salmon dry. Rub the salt and oil on it and leave it at room temperature for the surface to dry out a bit. Meanwhile, prepare a medium fire (350° to 375°F) in a charcoal grill, using the direct-heat grilling method (see page 14). When the grill reaches the desired temperature, remove the cedar plank from the water, wipe it thoroughly dry, place the plank on the grate, and char it on one side for 5 to 7 minutes (you'll hear some cracking and popping). Turn the plank over so the charred side is up, place the salmon on the plank, and put the plank on the grate. Cover and cook until the internal temperature registers 145°F in the thickest part, about 20 minutes. Remove the plank from the grill and let cool to slightly warmer than room temperature.

To arrange the salad: With the salmon on the plank, arrange all of the salad ingredients around the fish in separate mounds or small bowls. To compose a bite, place a lettuce leaf on your cupped palm, put a little bit of the fish and a few pieces of each of the other salad ingredients into it, and then top it with a teaspoon or so of the dressing. Now gather the edges of the lettuce into a purse and enjoy the whole bite at once.

DRESSING

4 to 6 fresh red bird's eye chiles, or 2 or 3 larger red hot chiles

4 large garlic cloves

⅓ cup fish sauce

⅓ cup packed grated palm sugar or granulated coconut sugar, or ¼ cup packed light brown sugar

½ cup fresh lime juice

FISH

1 (1-pound) salmon fillet

2 teaspoons salt

1 tablespoon vegetable oil

SALAD

1 cup unsalted roasted peanuts

4 ounces fresh ginger, peeled and cut into ¼-inch dice

4 ounces shallots, cut into ¼-inch dice

2 green Thai long chiles or jalapeños, thinly sliced (optional)

¾ cup firmly packed fresh cilantro leaves

¾ cup firmly packed fresh Thai or common basil leaves

¾ cup firmly packed fresh mint leaves

24 to 32 Bibb lettuce leaves

2 small, thin-skinned limes, unpeeled, cut into ¼-inch dice

HERB-FILLED GRILLED FISH

with Spicy Tamarind Dipping Sauce

SAUCE

½ cup tamarind paste
(see Note, page 23)

2 tablespoons fresh lime juice

2 tablespoons packed
grated palm sugar or
granulated coconut sugar,
or 1 tablespoon packed
light brown sugar

1 tablespoon red pepper
flakes

¼ cup fish sauce

FISH

4 whole striped bass, about
1½ pounds each, gutted
and scaled

2½ tablespoons kosher salt

2 cups loosely packed
hand-torn fresh leafy
herbs (such as Thai basil,
Vietnamese coriander,
mint, dill, cilantro, sawtooth
coriander [which is also
called culantro] or lemon
basil)

4 tablespoons vegetable oil

Cooked long-grain rice,
for serving

Grilled whole fish can be found throughout Southeast Asia, but this version from Myanmar (Burma), known as *nga kin*, is one of the simplest. It is also the best thing my friends and I ate during our first visit there when we crossed the border from Thailand's northern province of Mae Hong Son into Myanmar in the late 1990s, a time when tourism in that area wasn't booming as it is now. Whole freshwater fish, which had been stuffed with assorted fresh herbs and grilled over charcoal until charred and smoky, and rice formed the simple meal that our host put on the table for us. Maybe that modest yet glorious meal tasted so good because we arrived tired and hungry. What I do know is that this simple grilled fish is a reminder that when the freshest ingredients are on hand, there's not much else you need to do except get out of the way and let those ingredients shine.

At home, I like to use striped bass in this recipe. Red snapper is also a good option. Regardless of what fish you use, make sure it's absolutely fresh. Be creative with the herbs, but stick with two or three different types and no more, or the flavors will be muddled. This is a case where more isn't better. I like the pungent herb known in Thailand as *phak phaeo* or *phak phai* (*Percicaria odorata*) because it was one of the herbs I remember from my first encounter with *nga kin*. The herb is sold in the US as Vietnamese coriander or *rau răm*, and it can be found fresh in the produce section of most stores that sell Southeast Asian ingredients.

── ⌐ **SERVES 4**

To make the sauce: In a small saucepan, combine the tamarind paste, lime juice, sugar, pepper flakes, and fish sauce and bring to a boil over medium heat, stirring to dissolve the sugar and blend the ingredients. Simmer for 1 minute, then transfer to a small heatproof serving bowl. Set aside to cool.

Prepare a medium-high fire (400° to 450°F) in a charcoal grill using the two-zone method (see page 11).

To make the fish: Pat the fish dry with paper towels. Make three or four diagonal slits, each about ¼ inch deep, on both sides of each fish. Using 1 tablespoon of the salt, rub one-fourth of it into the cavity of each fish, then stuff each cavity with ¼ cup of the herbs. Tie each fish closed with kitchen string, making a series of loops spaced 1 inch apart to keep the herbs inside.

>> CONTINUED

Rub 1 tablespoon of the oil on each fish, coating both sides, and then rub the fish on both sides with the remaining 1½ tablespoons salt, dividing it evenly.

When the coals are covered with white ash and the grate is hot, oil the grate thoroughly. Place the fish on the hot side of the grill and cook, uncovered, until the skin is charred and crisp on the bottom, 5 to 7 minutes. (Putting the fish on the hot side first prevents them from sticking to the grate.) Flip the fish and cook until the second side is charred and crisp, 5 to 7 minutes. Use a spatula (a fish spatula works well) to flip the fish gently—to keep the herbs inside and prevent the skin from tearing—but swiftly and decisively. Use a second spatula if needed. Once both sides are charred, move the fish to the hold side of the grill, close the lid, and cook with the vents half-opened until the thickest part registers 140°F, 20 to 25 minutes.

Remove the fish from the grill and leave them to cool for 10 minutes. Remove and discard the strings and the herbs, and top the fish with the remaining fresh herbs. Serve the fish immediately with rice and the dipping sauce on the side.

NOTE >———————

Tamarind paste, also called tamarind concentrate, is the softened pulp of sour tamarind that has been slightly diluted with water. It comes in a plastic jar and is available at most Asian stores and online. Be sure to use a Thai or Vietnamese brand, as it has the right consistency and level of concentration for my recipes.

GRILLED FISH
with Fresh Herbs in Banana Leaf Packets

Kanap pa, a classic Lao dish also popular across the Mekong in northeastern Thailand, has many variations. This one is among the simplest and the best. You can serve it the traditional way with warm sticky rice, which calls for pinching off just enough to knead with your fingers into a bite-size oblong nugget, then using it to scoop up a mouthful of the fish and the juice. Or you can serve the fish over a plate of jasmine rice.

Lemon basil (sometimes called lime basil) is difficult to find even when you live in an urban area with large Asian stores selling specialty Southeast Asian produce. For this reason, I grow it in the summer. If you can't find it, Thai basil or common basil works fine.

SERVES 4

Prepare a medium-high fire (400° to 450°F) in a charcoal grill using the two-zone method (see page 11).

Before you begin making the packets, see page 85 for tips on purchasing and handling banana leaves. Lay the banana leaf squares in a single layer on a work surface. Rub the salt on the fish, dividing it evenly between the fillets, then place a fillet in the center of each banana leaf square.

Trim off the tough outer leaves and the root end from each lemongrass stalk. Beginning from the root end, use a very sharp knife to cut each bulb into paper-thin slices (it's very important for the slices to be very thin or they will be unpleasant to eat), stopping when the purple rings disappear. Top the fish fillets with the lemongrass slices, shallots, chiles, dill, lemon basil, and lime leaves (if using), dividing each ingredient evenly among the fillets.

Fold the right side of a banana leaf square over the fish, covering as much of it as you can, then fold the left side over the fish to overlap. Fold the top down and then fold the bottom up. Flatten the packet to even out the thickness of the fish mound. Secure the packet with a wooden toothpick. Repeat to make three more packets.

When the coals are covered with white ash and the grate is hot, place the packets, seam side up, on the hot side of the grill. Cover and cook with the vents half-opened until the internal temperature registers 120°F, 15 to 20 minutes. Uncover the grill and continue to cook until the internal temperature registers 140°F and the leaves are well charred (but not burned or collapsing), about 10 minutes longer.

Remove the packets from the grill and open them. Serve the fish in the packets, with the rice on the side.

4 (8-inch square) pieces banana leaf

4 teaspoons kosher salt

4 skinless mild-flavored fish fillets (such as sea bass, halibut, salmon, orange roughy, cod, or tilapia), about 8 ounces each

2 fat lemongrass stalks

2 ounces shallots, halved lengthwise, then thinly sliced lengthwise

8 to 10 fresh red bird's eye chiles, coarsely chopped, or 3 or 4 fresh red serrano or jalapeño peppers, sliced ⅛-inch thick

¼ cup loosely packed dill sprigs

¼ cup loosely packed fresh lemon basil leaves

2 tablespoons tightly packed deveined and very finely sliced makrut lime leaves (optional)

Cooked sticky rice (see page 56) or jasmine rice, for serving

GRILLED BABY OCTOPUS
with Spicy Peanut Sauce

4 pounds fresh baby octopuses, about 4 to 6 ounces each, thawed if frozen

1 head garlic, cloves separated and peeled

8 to 10 fresh bird's eye chiles, or 3 or 4 serrano or jalapeño peppers, thinly sliced

1 cup packed grated palm sugar or granulated coconut sugar, or ¾ cup packed light brown sugar

⅓ cup fish sauce

½ cup fresh lime juice

¼ cup vegetable oil

⅓ cup unsalted roasted peanuts, coarsely chopped

¼ cup coarsely chopped cilantro leaves and stems

In the past several years, sightings of itinerant vendors selling *pla muek yang* (grilled dried squid) have become few and far between in Thailand. That's such a shame. Of all the food vendors who come to customers on a bicycle—a motorbike these days—few are more fun to watch. They are hard to miss, too, as they arrive with a surprisingly large display panel of squid in various sizes—butterflied and dried—hanging in multiple, neatly overlapping rows looking much like heavily loaded clotheslines.

The process begins with you picking a squid you want and handing it to the vendor. He heats it up on a small charcoal grill until it is smoky and lightly charred, and then he feeds it into a hand-cranked squid-rolling machine (a bit like a pasta machine) outfitted with two ridged rollers. As the handle is cranked, the two rollers simultaneously stretch the squid to three or four times its original length while their ridged surfaces tenderize it, making it easy for you to tear off a bite-size piece and dip it into the ever-present sweet, sour, and spicy sauce specked with roasted peanuts.

It would be difficult to make grilled dried squid palatable—even chewable—without that piece of equipment, so here's a variation made with fresh baby octopus, which my friends and I like just as much as the original inspiration.

⎯⎯⎯⎯⎯⎯⎯⎯⎯⎯⎯⎯⎯⎯⎯⎯⎯⎯ ⟨ **SERVES 4**

Unless the octopuses have been cleaned, remove the heads. If you like to eat the head (I do), keep each one but remove the eyes, make a slit through each head, and remove and discard the internal organs. Flip each octopus over to locate the beak in the middle where the tops of the tentacles meet. Use the tip of a knife to make a circular cut around the beak. Squeeze the octopus and the beak will pop out. Rinse the octopus well, flushing out the head cavity and the eye sockets (if you keep the head) and making sure the suckers on the tentacles are clean.

Put the cleaned octopuses in a large saucepan and add water to cover by 2 inches. Bring to a boil over medium-high heat, reduce the heat to a gentle simmer, and cook to your preferred level of tenderness, from 30 minutes to over 1 hour. Thai people like their cephalopods on the chewy side; you may prefer them fork-tender. Testing for tenderness by sliding a knife into the area near the head (if you have kept it) or into where the tentacles meet.

▸▸ CONTINUED

Meanwhile, make the dipping sauce: In a small food processor or a mortar, blend the garlic and chiles until the bits are the size of a match head. Transfer to a small bowl, add the sugar, fish sauce, and lime juice and stir until the sugar dissolves. Set aside until serving.

Light a full chimney of charcoal. When the coals are ready, spread them out on the bottom of a kettle grill or hibachi for cooking over direct high heat (500° to 650°F).

When the octopuses are done, drain, pat dry, and moisten them evenly with the oil. When the coals are covered with white ash and the grate is hot, place the octopuses on the grate and cook, turning as needed, until lightly charred on all sides, 7 to 8 minutes total.

Remove the octopuses from the grill, separate the tentacles, and arrange on a platter. Finish the sauce by stirring in the peanuts and cilantro. You can drizzle the sauce over the tentacles or serve it in a bowl for dipping. Serve immediately.

SMOKED SHRIMP

with Chile-Lime Dipping Sauce

8 pounds jumbo (21 to 25 per pound) or extra-jumbo (16 to 20 per pound) shrimp, left whole

1 tablespoon salt

1 tablespoon ground white or black pepper

DIPPING SAUCE

15 green bird's eye chiles, or 8 jalapeño or serrano peppers, sliced

15 cloves garlic

1 cup fresh lime juice

1 teaspoon salt

1 teaspoon granulated sugar

¼ cup fish sauce

¼ cup coarsely chopped cilantro leaves and stems

This dish is inspired by the smoked shrimp of Malaysia, *udang salai*, which is similar to the smoked shrimp of southern Thailand, *kung siap*. The preparation involves cooking whole shrimp—complete with the heads, shells, and tails—low and slow over wood, coconut husks, or wood charcoal. The shrimp traditionally used for this dish are not usually large, and after smoking, they crisp up and shrink to the point where you can eat each one whole—head, shell, and tail— in a single bite. Besides, trying to peel them to get to the meat inside is time-consuming and often futile. This is why smoked shrimp are more commonly used as an ingredient in a dish or relish, or eaten as a snack, rather than served as part of a meal.

I use a smoker and a sweet, mild wood like cherry or apple for these jumbo shrimp. The shrimp I choose are quite large, so I serve them as a full meal along with a spicy chile-lime dipping sauce. This is a peel-and-eat affair, which lends itself well to a cookout or an outdoor party. Make a large batch, lay out the smoked shrimp, seafood boil–style, on a paper-lined picnic table, set a bowl of sauce in the middle, and go to town.

SERVES 8

In a large bowl, mix the shrimp with the salt and pepper, coating them evenly. Cover and refrigerate for 3 hours.

Meanwhile, start the sauce: In a blender, combine the chiles, garlic, lime juice, and salt and blend until the bits are the size of a match head. Transfer to a small bowl, cover, and keep at room temperature.

Heat a smoker to 225°F. Rinse the seasoning off the shrimp and pat dry with paper towels. Place the shrimp in the smoker and smoke until they turn dark coral, 20 to 25 minutes.

While the shrimp are smoking, stir the sugar and fish sauce into the sauce, then taste and adjust the seasoning with more fish sauce if needed. Aim for sour and hot first, then salty and just a tad bit of sweetness. Stir in the cilantro.

Serve the shrimp with the sauce.

GRILLED STINGRAY

with Chile Paste on Banana Leaves

4 large dried Thai long chiles or guajillo chiles, cut into 1-inch pieces

4 lemongrass stalks

5 ounces shallots, cubed, plus thinly sliced shallots, for garnish

10 large garlic cloves

3 thumb-size pieces fresh ginger, peeled and sliced

6 to 8 fresh red bird's eye chiles

1 tablespoon Malaysian or Thai shrimp paste, or 2 tablespoons miso or fermented soybean paste (see headnote, page 97)

½ cup vegetable oil

¼ cup packed grated palm sugar or granulated coconut sugar, or 3 tablespoons packed light brown sugar

½ cup tamarind paste (see Note, page 23)

Salt

2 stingray or skate wings or mahi mahi fillets, about 1 pound each

4 (12-inch-square) pieces banana leaf

Cooked jasmine rice, for serving

4 calamansi (see Note, page 79) or 2 limes, halved

Ikan pari bakar sambal, stingray or skate smothered with chile paste and grilled on banana leaves, is what I seek out every time I travel in Malaysia and Singapore. It's a classic that is well loved by the locals, and it's easy to see why. Some say the taste and texture of stingray and skate are akin to those of a scallop, but I think stingray and skate are more like a cross between fish and lobster: mild, firm, with a little bit of bounciness yet still flaky.

While stingray is hard to find in the United States, skate is routinely served at high-end restaurants, and a quick search will reveal several online sources for it. If you have large Korean supermarkets in your area, check out their seafood departments, as chances are they sell fresh skate wings, cut up and ready to use. If you can't find or don't like skate or stingray, use any type of saltwater fillet (my favorite for this purpose is mahi mahi), which works well even though the taste is different.

Belacan, or Malaysian shrimp paste, is similar to *kapi*, or Thai shrimp paste, but it's drier and harder and is sold in a brick-like block rather than in a soft paste form in a tub. *Belacan* can be much harder to find in the United States, so, if you can't locate it, use Thai shrimp paste instead. If neither of them is available, go with miso or fermented soybean paste.

This dish is traditionally grilled on or wrapped in banana leaves to take advantage of the fragrance the leaves impart when charred.

⟨ SERVES 4

In a small bowl, combine the dried chiles with warm water to cover and let stand until softened, about 15 minutes. Squeeze the pieces dry and add to a small food processor. Trim off the tough outer leaves and the root end from each lemongrass stalk. Beginning from the root end, use a very sharp knife to cut each bulb into thin slices, stopping when the purple rings disappear.

Add the lemongrass to the processor along with the cubed shallots, garlic, ginger, fresh chiles, and shrimp paste. Process until smooth. Scrape the mixture into an 8-inch frying pan, add the oil, and fry over medium-high heat until fragrant, about 1 minute. Stir in the sugar and tamarind and continue to stir until the sugar dissolves. Taste and adjust the seasoning with salt. Remove from the heat.

Prepare a medium-high fire (400° to 450°F) in a charcoal grill using the two-zone method (see page 11).

Before you begin making the packets, see page 85 for tips on purchasing and handling banana leaves. Lay one piece of banana leaf on top of a second piece to make a double-strength wrapper, making sure the grain of one piece runs perpendicular to that of the other. Do the same with the remaining two banana leaf squares. Place a piece of fish in the center of each stacked set. Make a few slits on the stingray or skate wings (but not on the fish fillets, if using). Spread half of the paste over the top surface of each wing.

Fold the right side of a banana leaf square over the fish, covering as much of it as you can, then fold the left side over the fish to overlap. Fold the top down and then the bottom up. Flatten the packet to even out the thickness of the fish mound. Secure the packet with a wooden toothpick. Repeat to make one more packet.

When the coals are covered with white ash and the grate is hot, place the packets, seam side up, on the hold side of the grill. Cover the grill and cook with the vents half-opened until the internal temperature registers 130°F, 20 to 25 minutes. Open the packets and move the fish closer to the hot side of the grill. Re-cover and cook with the vents half-opened until the internal temperature registers 140°F for the fish fillets and 150°F for the stingray or skate wings and the leaves are well charred (but not burned or collapsing), 10 to 15 minutes longer.

Remove the packets from the grill. Top with the sliced shallots and serve immediately with the rice and calamansi.

GRILLED OYSTERS

with Crispy Shallots, Green Onion Oil, and Peanuts

When it comes to oysters—raw or cooked—I was never a believer. Things changed when I took the first of several trips to the port city of Danang, Vietnam. There I encountered *hau nuong mo hanh*, fresh, sweet oysters grilled over charcoal—hot, smoky, and still bubbling in their own juices—and topped with green onions, crispy fried shallots, and chopped roasted peanuts. The scent. The flavor. The contrasting textures. I'm a convert.

½ cup paper-thin shallot slices

¾ cup vegetable oil

2 green onions, thinly sliced

¾ teaspoon kosher salt

½ cup unsalted roasted peanuts

24 oysters in the shell, scrubbed clean

MAKES 24 OYSTERS

Set a fine-mesh sieve over a small heatproof bowl and put it near the stove. In a small frying pan, combine the shallots and oil over medium-low heat and heat slowly, stirring occasionally. When the shallots begin to sizzle, start stirring more frequently so they cook evenly (the pieces around the edge of the pan will brown first). When the shallots are golden brown and crisp, after 5 to 7 minutes, immediately pour the contents of the pan into the sieve. Set the sieve with the shallots aside. Immediately stir the green onions and salt into the hot oil, then set the oil aside.

Wipe the pan clean and return it to medium-low heat. Add the peanuts and toast, shaking the pan occasionally to prevent scorching, until fragrant and golden, about 10 minutes. Transfer to a plate to cool, then coarsely chop them and combine with the fried shallots.

Light a full chimney of charcoal. When the coals are ready, spread them out on the bottom of a kettle grill or hibachi for cooking over a medium-high fire (400° to 450°F).

Meanwhile, shuck the oysters: Hold a kitchen towel in your nondominant hand and use it to grasp the oyster firmly, cupped side down. Use the other hand to slide the tip of a shucking knife into the dark, rounded spot at the oyster's hinge, approaching it from the bottom. Twist the knife, applying firm pressure, to release the hinge. When the hinge is broken, there will be a light pop and the top shell will come loose. Run the knife blade from the hinge around the edge of the oyster shell to separate the halves completely, then slide the blade along the underside of the upper shell to dislodge any meat. Discard the top shell. Keep the oyster in the bottom shell along with the oyster liquor. Repeat with the remaining oysters.

When the coals are mostly covered with white ash but still glowing, quickly arrange the oysters on the grate. When the oyster liquor is bubbling around the edges, after 3 to 5 minutes, spoon the green onion mixture onto the oysters, dividing it evenly. Cook for 1 minute longer.

Quickly transfer the oysters to a large platter and top with the fried shallot–peanut mixture, dividing it evenly. Serve immediately.

GRILLED MACKEREL

with Three-Flavored Sauce

SAUCE

10 fresh bird's eye chiles,
or 5 jalapeño or serrano
peppers, thinly sliced

5 large garlic cloves

1 ounce shallots, cubed

3 cilantro roots, chopped, or
3 tablespoons finely chopped
fresh cilantro stems stripped
of leaves

¼ cup plus 2 tablespoons
vegetable oil

½ cup packed grated palm
sugar or granulated coconut
sugar, or ⅓ cup packed light
brown sugar

2 tablespoons granulated
sugar

¼ cup water

¼ cup fish sauce

¼ cup tamarind paste
(see Note, page 23)

4 whole mackerel or other
oily, full-flavored fish, about
1½ pounds each, gutted
and scaled

Fresh red hot chiles or bell
pepper, seeded, deveined,
and cut lengthwise into thin
strips, for garnish

Cooked jasmine rice,
for serving

Few dishes better exemplify the flavors of the food of central Thailand than mackerel and the salty, sweet, and sour sauce known in Thai as three-flavored sauce. Adored by Thais, short-bodied mackerel, or *pla thu* (*Rastrelliger brachysoma*), is perfect for this dish. I use Atlantic mackerel in Chicagoland because it's easy to find, though any oily, strong-flavored fish, such as sardines, will stand up well to the bold flavors of the sauce.

SERVES 4

Prepare a medium-high fire (400° to 450°F) in a charcoal grill using the two-zone method (see page 11).

While waiting for the grill to heat, make the sauce: In a small food processor, combine the chiles, garlic, shallots, and cilantro roots and pulse until a coarse paste with bits the size of a match head forms. In a 2-quart saucepan, heat 2 tablespoons of the oil over medium-high heat. Add the paste, stir, and fry until fragrant, about 1 minute. Add both sugars, the water, fish sauce, and tamarind and bring to a boil, stirring constantly. Lower the heat and simmer until the sauce is reduced to ¾ to 1 cup, about 5 minutes. Remove from the heat and let cool slightly.

Pat the fish dry with paper towels. Make four diagonal slits, each about ¼ inch deep, on both sides of each fish. Rub the remaining ¼ cup oil on both sides of the fish, dividing the oil evenly.

When the coals are covered with white ash and the grate is hot, oil the grate thoroughly. Place the fish on the hot side of the grill, cover, and cook with the vents half-opened until the skin is charred and crisp on the bottom, 5 to 7 minutes. Flip the fish and cook until the second side is charred and crisp, 5 to 7 minutes. When both sides are charred, move the fish to the hold side of the grill, close the lid, and continue to cook with the vents half-opened until the internal temperature in the thickest part registers 140°F, 20 to 25 minutes.

Transfer the fish to a large serving platter. Check the sauce. It should have a pourable consistency; if has become too thick on cooling, stir in some warm water to thin as needed. Pour the sauce over the fish, then garnish with chile strips. Serve immediately, with the rice on the side.

GRILLED SHRIMP SKEWERS
with Spicy Sweet-and-Sour Sauce

8 cups ice water

1 tablespoon baking soda

2 teaspoons salt

3¼ pounds large shrimp, peeled and deveined

SAUCE

8 large garlic cloves, finely chopped

½ cup canned tomato puree

¾ cup Thai Sriracha sauce (such as Shark or Sriraja Panich brand), or ½ cup American Sriracha sauce (such as Huy Fong brand, aka "rooster sauce")

¼ cup packed light brown sugar

2 tablespoons distilled white or cider vinegar

1 teaspoon salt

2 teaspoons cornstarch mixed with ¼ cup water

1 tablespoon red pepper flakes

¼ cup vegetable oil

2 Thai long chiles or jalapeños, thinly sliced, for garnish

This recipe is a spin-off of one of the most ubiquitous Thai street snacks: grilled meatballs glazed with spicy sweet-and-sour sauce. Instead of meatballs, however, this nontraditional version uses shrimp. Unlike Italian meatballs, which are light and tender, Asian-style meatballs are firm and bouncy. To give shrimp a similar snappy texture, I soak them in ice water to which I add a little baking soda.

—————————————————⟨ **SERVES 4 TO 6 AS AN APPETIZER**

If not using metal skewers, soak twelve 12-inch bamboo skewers in water to cover for 1 to 2 hours.

In a large bowl, combine the ice water, baking soda, and salt and stir until the baking soda and salt dissolve. Add the shrimp and, if necessary, weight them down with a bowl to keep them submerged.

Meanwhile, to make the sauce: In a 1-quart saucepan, combine the garlic, tomato puree, Sriracha sauce, sugar, vinegar, and salt and bring to a gentle boil over medium-high heat, stirring to dissolve the sugar. Lower the heat and simmer for 1 minute. Add the cornstarch slurry and cook, stirring constantly, for 1 minute longer. Taste and adjust the seasoning with sugar, vinegar, or salt if needed, aiming for an equally salty, sweet, and sour balance. Stir in the pepper flakes, then remove from the heat and let cool to room temperature.

Drain the shrimp, rinse with cold running water, and blot dry with paper towels. Thread the shrimp onto the soaked skewers.

Light a half-full chimney of charcoal. When the coals are ready, spread them out on the bottom of a kettle grill or hibachi for cooking over a medium-high fire (400° to 450°F).

When the coals are covered with white ash and the grate is hot, grill the shrimp, brushing them with the oil and flipping them once or twice, until charred and turning opaque in the center, 5 to 7 minutes.

Transfer the shrimp to a platter, spoon the sauce over the shrimp, and sprinkle the chiles on top. Serve immediately.

SMOKED FISH

with Rice, Fried Egg, and Tomatoes

4 whole trout or mackerel,
1 to 1¼ pounds each, gutted
and scaled

8 cups lukewarm water

¼ cup soy sauce

⅓ cup salt

½ cup packed dark brown
sugar

3 bay leaves

4 garlic cloves, smashed

1 tablespoon crushed
black peppercorns

¾ cup coconut or
cider vinegar

4 fresh red and/or green
bird's eye chiles, thinly sliced

2 tablespoons vegetable oil

Cooked long-grain rice,
for serving

4 fried eggs, for serving

4 plum tomatoes, seeded
and cut into ½-inch cubes

Soy sauce, for serving

According to my good friend Jess, who lives in Quezon City in the Philippines, *tinapa* (smoked fish) served with rice, a fried egg, cubed tomatoes, and a tiny bowl of chile vinegar makes the best *almusal* (breakfast). And whenever I visit him and his family, that glorious combo is indeed what we eat every morning. I have absolutely no complaint about that.

The simplest recipe for *tinapa* involves a salt-and-water brine and smoking with coconut husks under a tent of banana leaves. It's not uncommon for home cooks to add aromatics to the brine to enhance the overall flavor of the finished fish.

Jess prefers milkfish or scad, which are among the varieties used to make *tinapa* in the Philippines. I use any fresh local fish I can find. For me, that often means lake trout or brown trout, though other types of fish, such as mackerel, herring, or sardines, also work well. Fatty fish absorb smoke better than leaner fish and yield moist and tender yet firm meat.

Coconut husks are hard to find in most Western countries. Use wood chips or wood pellets (I prefer to use my pellet smoker for this recipe). For smoking trout, I typically use half alderwood and half applewood. Some of my recipe testers prefer hickory. It depends on what you like, so experiment with different combinations.

SERVES 4

Measure the thickness of the fish at the thickest point. The thickness, not the weight, of the fish will determine the brining time. Using 30 minutes for each inch of thickness, compute the brining time. Arrange the fish in a single layer in deep baking dish.

To make the brine, in a large bowl, combine the water, soy sauce, salt, and sugar and stir to dissolve the salt and sugar. Add the bay leaves, garlic, and peppercorns and stir to mix. Pour the brine over the fish, cover, and refrigerate for the computed brining time, stirring the brine and turning the fish over every 15 minutes or so.

Remove the fish from the brine, rinse well under cold running water, and pat the cavity and the outside dry with paper towels. Put a rack on

>> CONTINUED

a sheet pan, arrange the fish on the rack in a single layer, and refrigerate, uncovered, for 2 to 3 hours to dry out the skin. This helps smoke adhere to the skin better.

Meanwhile, in a small bowl, combine the vinegar and chiles. Cover and leave at room temperature.

Heat a smoker to between 130° and 150°F (the wood chips do not need soaking). Smoke the fish for 1 hour. Increase the heat to between 175° and 190°F and smoke until the internal temperature registers 160°F, about 2 hours longer.

Remove the fish from the smoker and brush them on both sides with the oil. Serve the fish with the rice, fried eggs, and tomatoes. Place the bowl of chile vinegar and some soy sauce on the side for anyone who wants them.

GRILLED LOBSTER TAILS
with Fish Sauce–Chile Butter

Ayutthaya is one of the most fascinating provinces in all of Thailand—not just the central region in which it's located. A once-mighty kingdom and center of international trade, it's steeped in history and now a popular destination among foreign and local tourists. But what visitors often overlook amid the many attractions and historical sites are the understated yet rich culinary offerings of this fertile, riverine province.

Chief among the many kitchen treasures Ayutthaya has to offer are *kung mae nam phao*, giant river prawns, each as large as a toddler's arm, grilled over charcoal. In the old days, whole prawns would be cooked in their shells right on the embers, but nowadays they're nearly always butterflied before grilling. That change is mostly for ease of consumption and to showcase the saffron-colored tomalley, which ensures a spectacular presentation.

And it's the abundance of custardy tomalley that makes giant river prawns a delicacy among the Thais, who eat them with rice and a spicy and tart dipping sauce (that Thai people love with any grilled or steamed fish or shellfish). The combination of the sweet prawn meat, the heady dipping sauce, the rice, and the tomalley—nature's cream sauce—restores your faith in this world.

I use lobster tails here, as lobsters are the closest substitute for the giant river prawns of central Thailand and the tails are easier to prepare than whole lobsters. The butter is not a traditional ingredient in Asia, but it helps approximate the taste of the tomalley and serves as a convenient vehicle for the spicy, tangy, funky sauce, which is traditionally served in a separate bowl. One thing we need to keep traditional, however, is to serve this dish with warm jasmine rice.

¾ cup unsalted butter, preferably high-butterfat European-style, at room temperature

¼ cup finely chopped fresh cilantro

8 garlic cloves, minced

4 to 6 fresh red bird's eye chiles, minced

1 tablespoon fish sauce

¼ teaspoon salt

Grated zest of 2 limes, plus 2 limes, halved, for serving

2 pounds lobster tails

Cooked jasmine rice, for serving

SERVES 4

In a small saucepan, combine the butter, cilantro, garlic, chiles, fish sauce, salt, and lime zest and set aside.

Butterfly the lobster tails: Put a lobster tail, shell side up, on a cutting board. Using sturdy kitchen shears, cut the shell lengthwise down the center, positioning the bottom blade directly under the shell and not in the meat and cutting all the way to the base of the tail. Using your thumbs and fingers, grab each side of the cut shell and gently pull the meat out

>> CONTINUED

and upward so it lifts off the bottom of the shell but is still attached at the tail fan. Lay the meat on top of the cut shell and squeeze together the two halves of the shell beneath the meat. Using a sharp knife, make a shallow slit lengthwise down the center of the meat, being careful not to cut all the way through. Repeat with the remaining lobster tails.

Prepare a medium-high fire (400° to 450°F) in a charcoal grill using the two-zone method (see page 11).

When the coals are covered with white ash and the grate is hot, place the lobster tails, meat side up, in the middle of the grill between the hot side and the hold side, cover, and cook with the vents half-opened until the shells turn red and become charred and the meat is firm and opaque, about 2 minutes. Turn the lobster tails over, positioning them on the hot side of the grill and cook, with the lid off, until the meat is firm, opaque, and lightly charred, about 2 minutes more.

Transfer the lobster tails, meat side up, to a large platter. Set the saucepan with the butter mixture on the hot side of the grill and heat until the butter has melted and the mixture begins to sizzle a bit around the edges.

Pour the sauce over the lobsters. Serve immediately with the rice and with the lime halves for squeezing over both the lobster tails and the rice as you eat them.

ROASTED CORNISH GAME HENS

with Coconut Rice and Chile Relish

Ayam kampong or *ayam kampung*—literally, "village chicken" in Malay and Indonesian, respectively—is the indigenous breed that has long been raised by households (mostly in rural areas nowadays) and widely consumed in many parts of Southeast Asia. Traditional recipes from these countries call for a much smaller, slimmer bird than the supermarket-variety chicken we're used to. And since these chickens are typically raised in open spaces, where they can roam freely, their meat is chewier than that of their farm-raised counterparts.

And that works well because Southeast Asians generally prefer meats with some chew to them—meats that fight back just a little when you bite into them. *Thai kai ban*, "home chicken" or "village chicken," is similar to *ayam kampong*, and wherever it's offered alongside the larger supermarket *kai nuea* (literally, "meaty chicken"), it always commands a higher price per pound.

In the United States, where village chickens aren't available, I usually go for pheasants, which are commonly raised in a wide, netted field where they can fly and forage. The ring-necked pheasant has especially lean yet tender and flavorful meat, with the right amount of chew— just like the village chicken. Unfortunately, pheasants aren't widely available, and only a handful of online retailers sell them. Cornish game hens, on the other hand, can be found at many grocery stores, and I call for them here. If you can find a pair of pheasants, however, they would be perfect.

These simple roasted birds are served with two classic Indonesian accompaniments, coconut rice (*nasi uduk*) and *sambal oelek*. You can make the latter from scratch following the instructions here, or you can buy it at most Asian stores and some mainstream supermarkets.

⊰ **SERVES 4 GENEROUSLY**

To prep the hens: Cut off the wing tips from each hen. Rub the salt evenly over the inside and outside of each bird, dividing the salt evenly. Cover and refrigerate for 24 hours.

Once the birds are in the refrigerator, combine the soy sauce, lime juice, garlic, peppercorns, and bay leaves in a small bowl and mix well. Cover and refrigerate for 24 hours.

≫ CONTINUED

GAME HENS

4 Cornish game hens, 1 to 1¼ pounds each, or 2 pheasants, 2 to 2½ pounds each

1 tablespoon kosher salt

½ cup soy sauce

½ cup fresh lime juice

4 large garlic cloves, smashed

2 teaspoons coarsely cracked white or black peppercorns

4 fresh bay leaves, or 2 dried bay leaves

½ cup vegetable oil

½ cup packed grated palm sugar or granulated coconut sugar, or ⅓ cup packed light brown sugar

4 lemongrass stalks, each smashed to split the bulb, then tied into a knot

COCONUT RICE

2 cups jasmine rice, rinsed until the water runs clear

2¾ cups water

1 lemongrass stalk, smashed to split the bulb, then tied into a knot

1 cinnamon stick

2 whole cloves

1 cup unsweetened full-fat coconut milk

SAMBAL OELEK

8 to 12 fresh red bird's eye chiles

1 ounce shallots, cubed

3 garlic cloves

2 teaspoons vegetable oil

¼ teaspoon kosher salt

½ teaspoon granulated sugar

1 to 2 tablespoons fresh lime juice

Before roasting the birds, prepare the glazes. Strain the soy sauce mixture through a fine-mesh sieve into a small bowl, discarding the solids. Pour half of the strained mixture into a second small bowl. Stir half of the oil into one bowl (Glaze 1); add the remaining half of the oil and the palm sugar to the other bowl and stir until the palm sugar dissolves (Glaze 2). Set both bowls aside.

To make the rice: In a heavy 4-quart saucepan, combine the rice, water, lemongrass, cinnamon, and cloves and bring to a boil over medium-high heat, stirring often. Turn down the heat to low, cover the pot, and cook until the rice has absorbed most or all of the liquid, 15 to 20 minutes. Drizzle the coconut milk on top, turn down the heat to the lowest setting, re-cover the pot, and continue to cook for 10 minutes longer. The rice may still look too wet, but that's fine. Remove the pan from the heat, keep the cover on, and let the residual heat finish the cooking.

Prepare a medium-high fire (400° to 450°F) in a charcoal grill using the two-zone method (see page 11). While waiting for the coals to be ready, take the birds out of the refrigerator and dry them thoroughly on the outside with paper towels. Put a lemongrass stalk into the cavity of each hen (or 2 stalks into each pheasant). Tie the legs of each bird together with kitchen string.

When the coals are covered with white ash and the grate is hot, brush the birds with half of Glaze 1 and place them, on their sides, where the hold side of the grill meets the hot side. Cover and roast with the vents half-opened for 20 minutes. Turn the birds over so they rest on the other side and brush them with the remaining half of Glaze 1. Re-cover and roast with the vents half-opened for another 20 minutes. Reposition the birds so they are now lying on their backs, moving them farther away from the hot side of the grill. Brush them all over with Glaze 2. Re-cover and roast with the vents closed until the birds are golden brown and their internal temperature tested in the thigh away from bone registers 160°F, 10 to 15 minutes. Watch them closely during this last stage, as they can burn easily. Remove the birds from the grill and let rest for 15 minutes.

While waiting for the birds, quickly make the sambal: In a food processor or in a mortar and pestle, blend the chiles, shallots, and garlic to a coarse puree. In a small frying pan, heat the oil over medium heat. When the oil is hot, add the chile puree, salt, and sugar and fry until heated through and fragrant, about 1 minute. Transfer to a small serving bowl. Add 1 tablespoon of the lime juice. If the paste is still too thick, add more lime juice until it is the consistency of ketchup.

Fluff the rice, picking out and discarding the lemongrass, cinnamon, and cloves. Serve the roasted birds with the coconut rice and sambal.

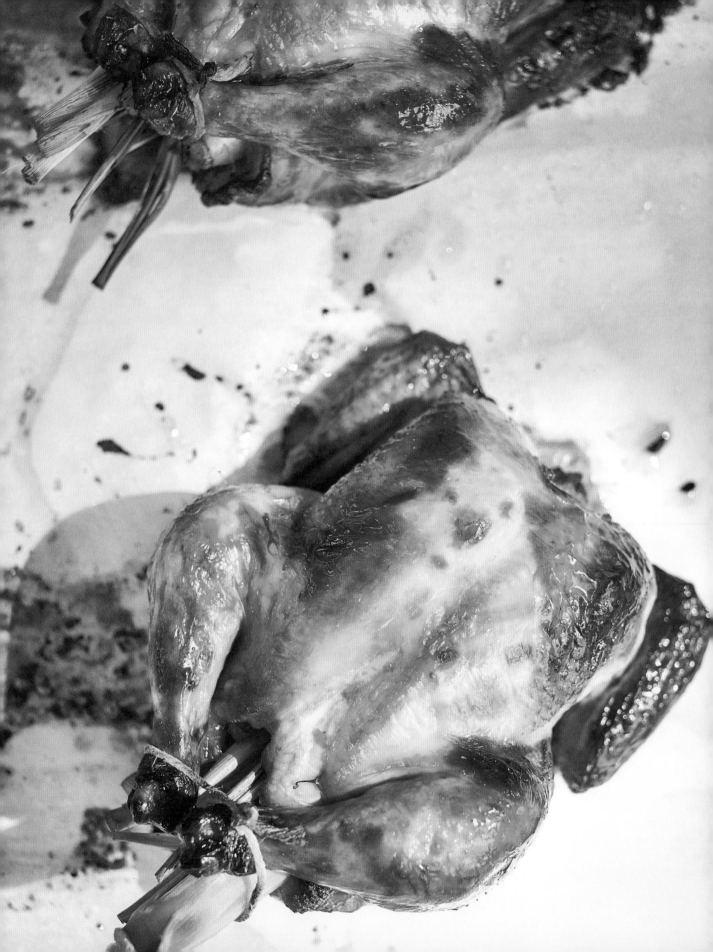

HOW TO SPATCHCOCK A BIRD

To spatchcock a bird (also called butterflying) is to cut it along its back and flatten it so it lies open like a book. The purpose is to reduce the grilling time and ensure even cooking. The latter is especially important because one of the age-old problems when cooking a whole bird is that the breasts can dry out by the time the legs are done.

Place the bird breast side down on a cutting board. Using a knife or kitchen shears and starting from the tail end, cut through the rib bones along both sides of the backbone to the head end. Set the backbone aside. Turn the bird breast side up and press down hard on the ridge of the breastbone to break it. Your bird is now lying flat in front of you, literally spineless. As for the backbone with the tail attached, you can keep it for making stock or, if you love eating skin and gnawing on bones like I do, cook it along with the body and consider it the cook's treat. This is the conventional Western method for spatchcocking a bird.

In Southeast Asia, however, birds are typically spatchcocked the opposite way. The cut is made on the breast side along one side of the breastbone and continues right through the wishbone (which gets removed). When the bird is flattened, the backbone and tail remain intact and the two breast halves are separated in the middle.

I've been asked many times why birds are spatchcocked this way in Southeast Asia, particularly in Thailand. I've relayed the question to other Thais, from local butchers and home cooks to people who make grilled chickens for a living. The responses I've received range from a blank stare and a series of rapid blinks to a quizzical look that says, Is there any other way to do it? Probed further, however, most agree with me that the main reason is because when a bird is spatchcocked this way you get to eat the whole bird, including the backbone and the tail, which many find the best parts. The concept of separating out the backbone and keeping it for making stock isn't part of the collective thought, especially because whole chicken carcasses are typically used for making stock, and they are widely available everywhere, including in supermarkets. On the other hand, calling dibs on that crisp, charred, and crunchy tail before your family members even realize it's being served is very much part of the family table.

One other advantage to making a cut between the breasts rather than along the backbone is that you don't run the risk of making the cuts too close to the thighs and losing "the oysters," the juicy, tender morsels of dark meat on either side of the backbone near the thigh. They are, for me, the second most delicious parts of the chicken.

For the recipes in this book, feel free to spatchcock your birds whichever way you like.

GRILLED CHICKEN AND SPICY CARROT SALAD

with Sticky Rice and Sweet Chile Sauce

CHICKEN

1 whole chicken, 3¼ to 3¾ pounds

3 lemongrass stalks

6 garlic cloves

2 cilantro roots, chopped, or 2 tablespoons finely chopped fresh cilantro stems stripped of leaves

2 teaspoons white or black peppercorns

1 ounce shallots, cubed

2 tablespoons fish sauce

2 tablespoons oyster sauce

3 tablespoons packed grated palm sugar or granulated coconut sugar, or 2 tablespoons packed light brown sugar

½ cup coconut oil

SWEET CHILE SAUCE

3 large garlic cloves

5 fresh red bird's eye chiles

¼ cup distilled white vinegar

¼ cup water

½ cup granulated sugar

1½ teaspoons salt

1 tablespoon cornstarch or potato starch mixed with 2 tablespoons water

STICKY RICE

2 cups Thai glutinous rice

The cuisine of Isan, the northeastern region of Thailand, covers a wide range of specialties, but the most widely celebrated of them all is the so-called trinity of Isan: grilled chicken (*kai yang*); a spicy salad (*som tam*), most commonly featuring green papaya; and cooked sticky rice (*khao niao*)—the triune ensemble that has won hearts and minds the world over.

In this version, the salad is made with carrots, once considered a novel cold-climate vegetable grown only in certain areas in Thailand but now a part of modern Thai cooking (papaya was foreign to Southeast Asia before it was introduced by European traders). I first tasted the salad twenty years ago at a carrot farm in the province of Phetchabun and since then have come to prefer it over the green papaya version.

The carrots must be grated into long, slender, crisp strands with sharp edges—unbruised and free of carrot juice flowing every which way. This is impossible to achieve with a box grater. The ideal tool is a julienne hand grater, which is easy to find, simple to use, and affordable (I like the Kiwi brand).

Be sure to purchase the correct kind of rice, which can be variously labeled "glutinous rice," "sweet rice," or "sticky rice" in English. This is the type that's widely consumed in Laos and Thailand, where it's cooked not in boiling water but in a basket set *above* boiling water. At Asian markets, look for an opaque white medium-grain rice imported from Thailand with the word ข้าวเหนียว somewhere on the package.

Making this set meal can seem overwhelming, but it's not difficult if you follow the suggested start times for each dish. Do the prep work for the salad in advance and refrigerate the fresh ingredients, so you can assemble the salad while the grilled chicken is resting.

─── ⟨ SERVES 4 TO 6

To make the chicken: Spatchcock the chicken (see page 55) and put it into a large bowl. Trim off the tough outer leaves and the root end from each lemongrass stalk. Beginning from the root end, use a very sharp knife to cut each bulb into thin slices, stopping when the purple rings disappear.

≫ CONTINUED

CARROT SALAD

2 large garlic cloves

3 or 4 fresh bird's eye chiles

1 tablespoon packed grated palm sugar or granulated coconut sugar, or 2 teaspoons packed light brown sugar, plus more as needed

2 tablespoons dried shrimp (see Note)

½ cup unsalted dry-roasted peanuts

¼ pound green beans, trimmed and cut into 1½-inch sticks

1 pound carrots (preferably the large, loose type), peeled and grated with a julienne hand grater into 3- to 4-inch-long strands

4 ounces cherry tomatoes, halved

3 tablespoons fresh lime juice

1 tablespoon fish sauce

2 tablespoons coarsely chopped unsalted dry-roasted peanuts, for garnish

NOTE >————————

Small shrimp that have been sundried and shelled are used in various Thai recipes and can be found at most Asian stores either in the dry goods section or in the refrigerator. Choose the type that's meaty with the shells and heads removed.

Measure out ⅓ cup, discarding the rest, and put it into a blender along with the garlic, cilantro roots, peppercorns, shallots, fish sauce, oyster sauce, and palm sugar. Process to a smooth paste. Scrape every bit of the marinade into the chicken bowl. Rub the marinade on the chicken, making sure to spread it over every bit of the skin and meat. Cover and refrigerate for at least 8 hours or up to overnight, occasionally turning the bird over and spooning the marinade that settles at the bottom of the bowl over it.

Meanwhile, prepare the sweet chile sauce: In a small food processor, blend the garlic, chiles, vinegar, and water until the garlic and chile bits are the size of a match head. Scrape the mixture into a 1-quart saucepan. Add the granulated sugar and salt and bring to a boil over medium-high heat, stirring until the sugar and salt dissolve. Turn down the heat to a gentle simmer and cook, uncovered, for 3 minutes. Whisk the cornstarch slurry into the sauce and cook, whisking constantly, until the sauce thickens slightly and becomes glossy, 1 to 2 minutes. Remove from the heat and leave to cool completely. Store in a tightly capped glass jar in the refrigerator for at least 8 hours or up to overnight.

To cook the sticky rice, you'll need to begin soaking it 8 to 12 hours before you plan to cook it. First, select a large fine-mesh stainless-steel sieve and a deep saucepan or stockpot with a circumference roughly the same as that of the sieve. Set the pan aside. Put the rice into the sieve and submerge the rice—sieve and all—in a large bowl of cold water to cover by 3 inches. Let stand at room temperature for 8 to 12 hours.

About 30 minutes before you begin to cook the chicken, start cooking the sticky rice. Lift the sieve from the bowl of water and, with the rice still in the sieve, rinse the rice under cold running water until the water runs clear; shake off the excess moisture. Rest the sieve in the rim of the reserved pan to see how low it sits, then remove the sieve and fill the pan with water to within about 3 inches of the bottom of where the sieve will reach. At no point should the rice touch the water. Place the sieve on the pan and cover the rice with a pot lid that can rest on the sieve without touching the rice. Set the pan over high heat and bring the water to a boil. Steam the rice, flipping it once after 10 minutes or so with a rubber spatula, until the grains are soft, translucent, glossy, and sticky yet remain distinct. This should take about 25 minutes. Transfer the rice to a lidded container to keep it warm while you cook the chicken.

Prepare a medium fire (350° to 375°F) in a charcoal grill using the two-zone method (see page 11). When the coals are covered with white ash and the grate is hot, place the chicken, bone side down, toward the hold side. Cover and cook with the vents half-opened, flipping the chicken and moving it back and forth between the hold side and the hot side every 10 minutes and adjusting the vents as needed to keep the chicken from burning before it has cooked through. The bird is ready when it is golden brown on both sides and the internal temperature in the thickest part of the thigh away from bone registers 155° to 160°F, about 45 minutes. Transfer it to a cutting board to rest, uncovered, for 30 minutes (during this time the temperature will continue to rise to about 165°F).

Meanwhile, make the salad: Put the garlic, chiles, and palm sugar into a large mortar and pound with a pestle until a paste forms. Add the dried shrimp and pound until they disintegrate. Add the peanuts, pounding until they are broken up into tiny pieces. Add the green beans and pound until they split, then stir to mix. Add the carrots and tomatoes, pounding just until the carrots are slightly softened and the tomatoes are bruised and release some juices; stir to mix. Add the lime juice and fish sauce and stir the contents of the mortar with a large spoon. Taste and add more lime juice, fish sauce, or sugar if needed. Aim for sour first, then salty, and then sweet. Transfer to a rimmed plate and top with the peanuts.

Cut the chicken into pieces and serve it immediately with the carrot salad, sticky rice, and sweet chile sauce.

LEMONGRASS GRILLED CHICKEN

with Crispy Garlic and Spicy Bamboo Shoot Salad

CHICKEN

1 whole chicken, 3½ to 3¾ pounds

2 lemongrass stalks

6 large garlic cloves

2 cilantro roots, roughly chopped, or 2 tablespoons finely chopped fresh cilantro stems stripped of leaves

3 teaspoons white or black peppercorns

2 tablespoons peeled and coarsely chopped fresh ginger

2 tablespoons grated makrut lime or regular lime zest

3 tablespoons soy sauce

2 tablespoons fish sauce

3 tablespoons packed grated palm sugar or granulated coconut sugar, or 2 tablespoons packed light brown sugar

BAMBOO SHOOT SALAD

3 tablespoons Thai glutinous rice (see headnote, page 56)

1 jar (1½ pounds) bamboo shoot strips in yanang juice

2 ounces shallots, halved lengthwise, then thinly sliced lengthwise

1 tablespoon fish sauce

¼ cup fresh lime juice

Red pepper flakes, for seasoning

⅓ cup coarsely chopped fresh cilantro leaves and stems

⅓ cup fresh mint leaves

2 tablespoons toasted white sesame seeds

Grilled chicken made in the tradition of Khao Suan Kwang, a village in northeastern Thailand, is one of the most sought-after iterations of the preparation in the entire country. It's not uncommon for people from other regions to take a trip to this small town just to experience it.

The dish looks deceptively simple, and first-timers are often disappointed that it's indistinguishable from the grilled local free-range chickens sold by vendors in rural markets throughout Isan. The small, lanky cockerels—their feet menacingly cupping—are secured between partially split madan (*Garcinia schomburgkiana*) wood and cooked over the most rudimentary grill setup imaginable—one more likely to inspire derision than awe.

Starting at the bottom, you've got *tao than*, the traditional Thai portable clay grill. Sitting atop it is *kalamang*, a large, white enameled bowl (the type used in rural areas to wash clothes and bathe babies) with its bottom removed. The bottomless bowl is just shy of a foot tall and has a flared top. A metal grate rests atop the bowl, and the chicken cooks on the grate.

And, oh, it works well in creating grilled chicken with golden brown skin—smoky and deeply flavorful. The washing bowl creates a distance between the glowing coals at the bottom of the clay grill and the chicken, preventing flare-ups and maintaining moderate heat, which is conducive to better absorption of smoke. Unless you have all of the components for this setup, you'll need to use a kettle grill, which works just fine.

I have chosen to pair the chicken with a spicy bamboo shoot salad (*sup no mai*) for a single simple reason: I love this pungent, flavorful Thai Lao salad. Being somewhat of an acquired taste, this classic warm salad is often overshadowed by *som tam*, its more internationally known papaya-based peer (a carrot version appears on page 58). To make a proper Isan bamboo shoot salad, you need to source the young bamboo shoots that come in a glass jar, with a label indicating the shoots are packed in the juice of *bai yanang*, the leaves of *Tiliacora triandra*, a plant native to mainland Southeast Asia. Most well-stocked grocery stores specializing in Southeast Asian ingredients and several online sources carry various brands of this imported product (Pantai and Maesri

>> CONTINUED

CRISPY GARLIC

1 head garlic, separated into
cloves and peeled

¾ cup vegetable oil

Cooked sticky rice
(see page 56), kept warm,
for serving

Sweet chile sauce
(see page 56), for serving

are great brands). You can use other types of unfermented bamboo products that are more widely available—be it those that come in long strips or in thin, rectangular pieces—but you'll need to lower your expectations as well, as the results will be miles away from what the Thais recognize as a good Isan bamboo shoot salad.

SERVES 4

To make the chicken: Spatchcock the chicken (see page 55) and put it into a large bowl. Trim off the tough outer leaves and the root end from each lemongrass stalk. Beginning from the root end, use a very sharp knife to cut each bulb into thin slices, stopping when the purple rings disappear. Measure out ⅓ cup, discarding the rest, and put it into a blender along with the garlic, cilantro roots, peppercorns, ginger, lime zest, soy sauce, fish sauce, and sugar. Process to a smooth paste. Rub the marinade on the chicken, making sure to spread it over every bit of the skin and meat. Cover and refrigerate for at least 8 hours or up to overnight, occasionally turning the bird over and spooning the marinade that settles at the bottom of the bowl over it.

About 1 hour before you begin to cook the chicken, prep the bamboo shoot salad: In a dry small frying pan, toast the rice over medium-low heat, stirring almost constantly, until the grains are golden brown and have a nutty aroma, about 15 minutes. Immediately transfer the rice to a small heatproof bowl and let cool completely (do not leave it in the pan, as it will continue to toast). In a small food processor or a mortar, grind the rice to a coarse powder, then set aside.

Empty the bamboo shoot jar—liquid and all—into a 4-quart saucepan (if the bamboo shoots aren't completely shredded into separate strands, shred them with a fork). Set aside.

To make the crispy garlic: Pound the garlic in a mortar (preferably) or grind in a small food processor into small chards, making sure all of the pieces are roughly equal in size and not small enough to turn into a fine paste. Set a fine-mesh sieve over a small heatproof bowl and set the bowl near the stove. In a small frying pan, combine the garlic and oil over medium-low heat and heat gently, stirring often. When the garlic turns light brown around the edge of the pan, start stirring more frequently to ensure even cooking (don't raise the heat). When the garlic is golden brown and crispy, immediately pour the contents of the pan into the sieve; set aside to cool. Keep the crispy garlic for a garnish and reserve the garlic oil for brushing on the chicken as it grills.

Prepare a medium fire (350° to 375°F) in a charcoal grill using the two-zone method (see page 11). When the coals are covered with white ash and the grate is hot, place the chicken, bone side down, near the center of the hold side. Cover and cook with the vents half-opened, flipping the chicken and moving it back and forth between the hold side and the hot side every 10 minutes and adjusting the vents as needed to keep the chicken from burning before it has cooked through. The bird is ready when it is golden brown on both sides and the internal temperature in the thickest part of the thigh away from bone registers 155° to 160°F, about 45 minutes. Transfer it to a cutting board to rest, uncovered, for 30 minutes (during this time the temperature will continue to rise to about 165°F).

While the chicken is resting, finish the bamboo shoot salad: Set the pan with the bamboo strands over medium heat, bring to a boil, and boil for 1 minute. Remove from the heat and stir in half of the rice powder, the shallots, fish sauce, and lime juice. Taste and adjust the seasoning with more fish sauce and lime juice as needed, aiming for equally salty and sour. Add as much pepper flakes as you like, stir well, and transfer to a rimmed plate. Top with the cilantro and mint. Sprinkle the remaining toasted rice powder and the sesame seeds over the top.

Cut the chicken into pieces and arrange on a platter. Sprinkle the crispy garlic on top and serve with the warm bamboo salad, sticky rice, and sweet chile sauce.

CLAY JAR CHICKEN
with Dried Chile-Tamarind Dipping Sauce

CHICKEN

8 cups warm water

½ cup soy sauce

¼ cup kosher salt

⅓ cup packed light brown sugar

½ cup Thai Sriracha sauce (such as Shark or Sriraja Panich brand), or ¼ cup American Sriracha sauce (such as Huy Fong brand, aka "rooster sauce")

4 cups very cold water

1 whole chicken, 3¼ to 3½ pounds

DIPPING SAUCE

1 tablespoon Thai glutinous rice (see headnote, page 56)

¼ cup tamarind paste (see Note, page 23)

¼ cup fish sauce

1 tablespoon packed light or dark brown sugar

2 tablespoons fresh lime juice

1 ounce shallots, thinly sliced lengthwise

¼ cup finely chopped fresh cilantro

One of the most fun outdoor cooking activities I have experienced both as an observer and an active participant is roasting meat—almost always chicken—inside a traditional Thai clay jar called an *ong*. A basket of hot, glowing coals rests on the inside bottom of the large jar (thirty to fifty gallons in capacity) and meat hangs over the coals from the rim of the opening at the top. The setup is comparable to a South Asian tandoor, a Central Asian *tonur*, or various other outdoor clay ovens that are used by cultures around the globe. They all produce similar results.

The difference, however, lies in the "off-label" use of the Thai *ong*, which has historically not been used for anything else other than to store rainwater—a practice that continues to this day in rural areas. Even today—at least two decades since *kai op ong* (chicken roasted in an *ong*) became a thing in small circles—the idea of using it as cooking equipment still seems novel. It's the same feeling I had when I was once invited to a pig roast at a friend's house and saw how he had turned an old porcelain bathtub into a roasting pit.

Strange or not, this setup produces great roasted chickens. The hook-and-hang method allows the juices of the meat and the seasonings to drip onto the coals below and create smoke that floats upward to perfume the meat. At the same time, the airflow inside the jar ensures that birds are heated from all sides at once, which is what makes a chicken cooked in a clay jar much smokier and juicier than one prepared on a regular charcoal grill.

Meathead Goldwyn, author of *Meathead: The Science of Great Barbecue and Grilling*, explains that in order to replicate the effects of the clay jar, you need a roaster with thick ceramic walls that will absorb a large amount of heat and radiate it back at the birds. The best substitute for the *ong*, he says, is a ceramic kamado grill (see page 6). Even though you don't hang the chicken inside the kamado the way you do inside the Thai clay jar, the shape of the kamado and the position of the coals ensure the same results.

In a nod to the clay jar chicken of Thailand, I suggest flavoring the chicken the way most vendors do: brining it and then applying an aromatic paste just before cooking.

SERVES 4

To brine the chicken: In a 4-quart saucepan, combine the warm water, soy sauce, salt, sugar, and Sriracha and bring to a gentle boil over medium heat, stirring just until the salt and sugar dissolve. Remove from the heat and let cool to room temperature. Stir in the cold water.

Put the chicken into a 2-gallon (jumbo) ziptop plastic bag, carefully pour in the brine, press out the air, and seal the bag closed. Put the bag into a large bowl and refrigerate, turning the bag occasionally, for at least 8 hours or up to overnight.

Meanwhile, get a head start on the dipping sauce: In a dry small frying pan, toast the rice over medium-low heat, stirring almost constantly, until the grains are golden brown and have a nutty aroma, about 15 minutes. Immediately transfer the rice to a small heatproof bowl and let cool completely (do not leave it in the pan because it will continue to toast). In a small food processor or a mortar, grind the rice to a coarse powder, then set aside.

In a small saucepan, combine the tamarind, fish sauce, and sugar and cook over medium heat, stirring, just until the mixture bubbles lightly around the edges and the sugar dissolves. Remove from the heat and leave it to cool in the pan for now.

Just before the chicken has finished brining, prepare a kamado grill for indirect cooking according to the manufacturer's instructions, setting it at 350°F.

While the grill is heating, prepare the aromatics: In a small food processor or a mortar, combine the garlic, cilantro roots, peppercorns, coriander, and turmeric and grind to a smooth paste. Take the chicken out of the brine and discard the brine. Rinse the chicken inside and outside under cold running water (being careful to minimize the chances of kitchen contamination) and blot it dry with paper towels. Rub the paste all over the outside. Slip the lemongrass knots into the cavity, tuck the wings back, and tie the legs together with kitchen string.

Place the chicken, breast side up, on the hold side of the grill and grill until the skin is golden brown and crisp and the internal temperature in the thickest part of a thigh away from bone registers 155° to 160°F, about an hour. Tent the breast if it begins browning too much before the bird is cooked through. Transfer the chicken to a cutting board to rest, uncovered, for 20 minutes (during this time the temperature will continue to rise to about 165°F).

While the chicken is resting, finish the dipping sauce: Stir the lime juice, shallots, and half of the cilantro into the mixture in the saucepan, then scrape the mixture into a small bowl. Top with the ground toasted rice and the remaining half of the cilantro.

Carve the chicken and serve with sticky rice and the dipping sauce.

AROMATICS

4 large garlic cloves

2 cilantro roots, roughly chopped, or 2 tablespoons chopped fresh cilantro stems stripped of leaves

2 teaspoons white or black peppercorns

2 teaspoons coriander seeds

2 teaspoons ground turmeric

2 lemongrass stalks, each smashed to split the bulb, then tied into a knot

Cooked sticky rice (see page 56), for serving

HAY-SMOKED CHICKEN

CHICKEN

4 quarts water

½ cup fish sauce

¼ cup soy sauce

½ cup kosher salt

1 cup packed grated palm sugar or granulated coconut sugar, or ¾ cup packed light brown sugar

4 quarts very cold water

1 whole chicken, 3¼ to 3¾ pounds

AROMATIC PASTE AND RUB

6 large garlic cloves

1 tablespoon white or black peppercorns

2 cilantro roots, chopped, or 2 tablespoons finely chopped fresh cilantro stems stripped of leaves

2 tablespoons vegetable oil

2 teaspoons ground turmeric

2 teaspoons ground coriander

2 pounds Timothy hay

Cooked sticky rice (see page 56), for serving

Sweet chile sauce (see page 56), for serving

The traditional Thai way of making hay-smoked chicken, or *kai op fang*, sounds more romantic than it really is. It involves standing a chicken upright on a stake (like a beer-can chicken without the can or the beer), covering it with an empty kerosene tin with one end removed, enveloping the whole setup with copious amounts of hay, and setting it all on fire. This is why it's only done on rural farms with no neighbors within a visible radius and by people who are experienced—or drunk—enough, given the erratic nature of the heat produced this way.

Setting your backyard on fire makes for a dramatic cookout party trick, and some people will tell you that you need to do just that to create the best Thai-style hay-smoked chicken. But, you see, the whole point is to perfume the chicken as it cooks with the intoxicating scent of burnt hay, and the traditional method isn't the only way to achieve that goal. I've been using this safer, more convenient, more reliable, and environmentally friendlier method for years to create even better chickens. No burnt patches in my lawn. My insurance agent still talks to me. And so do my neighbors. You'll need a 6- to 7-quart cast-iron Dutch oven and a kettle grill large enough to accommodate the pot.

I get fresh, clean hay from a farm close to my home. If you don't live near such a farm, clean Timothy hay (dried Timothy grass) from a pet store is your best bet—that is, if you're okay with some bunnies or other grass-eating animals giving you side-eye on the way out.

───────────────────────────────────────⟨ SERVES 4

To brine the chicken: In an 8-quart stockpot, combine the water, fish sauce, soy sauce, salt, and sugar and bring to a gentle boil over medium-high heat, stirring just until the salt and sugar dissolve. Remove from the heat and let cool to room temperature. Stir in the cold water. Put the chicken into the brine and top it with a large bowl with a heavy food can in it to keep it submerged. Refrigerate overnight.

About 2 hours before the chicken goes on the grill, make the aromatic paste: In a small food processor or a mortar, combine the garlic, peppercorns, and cilantro roots and grind to a smooth paste. Remove the chicken from the brine and discard the brine. Rinse the chicken inside and outside under cold running water (being careful to minimize the chances of kitchen contamination) and blot it dry with paper towels. Rub the paste inside the cavity, keeping the skin clean. Rub the oil all over the outside of the bird, coating the skin evenly. Mix together the turmeric and coriander in a small

>> CONTINUED

dish and then rub it evenly over the oiled skin. Leave the chicken at room temperature for 2 hours.

Prepare a medium-high fire (400° to 450°F) in a charcoal grill using the two-zone method (see page 11). Soak 1 pound of the hay in water to cover.

Line a 6- to 7-quart cast-iron Dutch oven with the remaining dry hay. Tuck the chicken's wings back and tie the legs together with kitchen string. Place the chicken, breast side up, on the hay. When the coals are covered with white ash and the grate is hot, put the Dutch oven, uncovered, on the hold side of the grill. Cover the grill and, with the vents half-opened, cook, keeping the grill temperature between 350° and 375°F, until the internal temperature in the thickest part of the breast away from bone registers 160°F, about 1 hour.

Remove the Dutch oven from the grate and then remove the grate. Spread the coals evenly over the bottom of the grill and place the Dutch oven directly on the coals. Remove the soaked hay from the water, shaking off the excess water, and drop it into the hot coals surrounding the pot. Immediately close the grill lid (but leave the Dutch oven uncovered) to trap the smoke inside and leave for 5 to 7 minutes.

Remove the Dutch oven from the grill and let the chicken rest for 20 minutes. Carve the chicken and serve with the sticky rice and sweet chile sauce.

SMOKING IN SOUTHEAST ASIA

One of the misconceptions about Southeast Asian cooking — and I've heard this several times — is that smoking isn't part of its culinary tradition. Although it's true that there is not yet a strong DIY culture, and smoking is largely limited to artisans and food manufacturers, preserving food through smoking has always been done in this part of the world.

The tools and the setups are different from what you may know. In other words, you probably won't see a cedar smokehouse in Southeast Asia. But an arrangement that allows, for example, fish under a blanket of edible leaves to cook slowly over coals or wood billowing blue smoke is common.

The fuels, of course, are different, too. People in every culture traditionally use whatever is growing nearby for their smoking fuel. That means that just as alder, hickory, apple, pecan, cherry, mesquite, and the like are used for smoking in North America, bagasse, coconut husks, dried corncobs, mangrove wood, rambutan wood, white popinac wood, hay, rubber wood sawdust, and other readily accessible sources are used in Southeast Asia.

GHEE-SMOKED CHICKEN AND RICE

with Spicy Mint Sauce

When my paternal grandparents moved into their new home in the Min Buri District, on the east side of Bangkok—a dream home away from the city center with enough acreage to plant as many mango trees as they wanted—they found themselves living amid several communities of Thai Sunni Muslims, who had been settled in the area for generations. At first it was a new experience for my grandparents. Being roused from sleep before dawn by multiple loudspeakers announcing the first call for prayer had never before been part of their daily routine, for example. But it didn't take them long to adjust to the new environment and to get to know and appreciate the new neighbors. In fact, my grandmother became close friends with several elderly ladies from these communities, who would sometimes go to her house and play board games with her on weekdays when she was home alone. Things developed from there. The board game group quickly became a book club, a knitting club, an orchid-growing club, and eventually a lunch club, where the members took turns cooking a dish for the group and teaching the other members how to make it.

This recipe started from chicken biryani, a classic South Asian chicken and rice dish that Fatima, one of the lunch club members, got from her Pakistani mother-in-law, who had settled in Thailand. Looking at the ingredients, I can tell that Fatima's mother-in-law must have simplified it a great deal, as it barely resembles chicken biryani as it is traditionally made in South Asia. Maybe several key South Asian ingredients weren't widely available in Thailand when she immigrated. Or maybe Fatima's mother-in-law was just having fun with it. Regardless, it was a favorite among the lunch club ladies.

Fatima cooked marinated chicken thighs on a charcoal grill and nestled them in a bed of fried rice before smoking the finished dish using the *dhungar* method (see page 77), which imparted the smoky, buttery scent that my grandmother remembered. She used Thai jasmine rice instead of basmati rice, which is typically used in South Asian cooking, and served the dish with her own hot and tangy mint sauce.

CHICKEN

4 large bone-in, skin-on chicken thighs

¼ cup plain full-fat yogurt (not Greek yogurt)

1 tablespoon peeled and minced fresh ginger

1 tablespoon minced garlic

1 tablespoon Madras curry powder

1 teaspoon salt

1 teaspoon cayenne pepper

SAUCE

12 fresh green bird's eye chiles, or 6 large green serrano or jalapeño peppers, sliced

½ cup firmly packed fresh mint leaves

½ cup firmly packed fresh cilantro leaves

2 teaspoons granulated sugar

¼ teaspoon salt

½ cup fresh lime juice

⤚ **SERVES 4 GENEROUSLY**

To marinate the chicken: Make two or three evenly spaced gashes on the meaty side of each chicken thigh. In a large bowl, combine the yogurt, ginger, garlic, curry powder, salt, and cayenne and mix well. Add the chicken and turn to coat evenly. Cover and refrigerate for 4 to 6 hours.

≫ CONTINUED

FRIED RICE

¾ cup vegetable oil

2 ounces shallots, halved lengthwise, then thinly sliced lengthwise

3 large garlic cloves, minced

4 large fresh red hot chiles, or 1 small red bell pepper, seeded, deveined and cut into ¼-inch dice

½ cup golden or dark raisins, soaked in water to cover for 15 minutes, drained, and blotted dry

1 tablespoon chicken bouillon granules

1 tablespoon Madras curry powder

2 teaspoons ground turmeric

1 teaspoon salt

4 cups packed cooked jasmine rice, separated into individual grains

¼ cup ghee, melted

Just before you light the grill, make the sauce: In a blender, combine the chiles, mint, cilantro, sugar, salt, and lime juice and blend until not quite smooth; tiny bits of the ingredients should be visible. Taste and adjust the seasoning with more salt and lime juice if needed, aiming for sour, sweet, and very spicy notes. Set aside at room temperature until serving time.

Start the fried rice by frying the shallots: Put a fine-mesh sieve over a small heatproof bowl. In a small frying pan, combine the oil and shallots over medium heat and cook, stirring constantly, until the shallots are golden brown and crispy, 5 to 7 minutes. Immediately pour the contents of the pan into the sieve. Let the shallots and oil cool separately.

Prepare a medium-high fire (400° to 450°F) in a charcoal grill using the two-zone method (see page 11).

While the coals are heating, finish the fried rice: In a large wok or frying pan, heat 2 tablespoons of the shallot-flavored oil over high heat. Add the garlic and chiles and fry until the chiles have softened a bit, about 1 minute. Stir in the raisins, bouillon granules, curry powder, turmeric, and salt and fry just until the spices are dispersed (if the pan is too dry, add a few tablespoons of water). Add the rice and stir-fry until heated through and the rice is evenly tinted yellow, 1 to 2 minutes. Transfer to a Dutch oven or other large, heavy pot with a tight-fitting lid. Put the ghee in a small heatproof container and place it in the middle of the rice, pushing down slightly to make sure it stays in place and won't tip over. Put the lid on the pot to keep the rice warm.

When the coals are covered with white ash and the grate is hot, oil the grate thoroughly. Place the chicken in the center of the grill between the hot side and the hold side. Cook the thighs with the vents half-opened, flipping them and moving them back and forth between the hold side and the hot side every 3 to 5 minutes. Along the way, brush them with the remaining shallot oil, being careful of flare-ups. The chicken pieces are ready when they are golden brown and the internal temperature in the thickest part of a thigh away from bone registers 165°F, about 30 minutes.

Using tongs, transfer the chicken pieces to the rice pot, arranging them around the ghee container and pushing them down into the rice—or even burying them in the rice. Take one or two pieces of burning charcoal from the grill and place them in the ghee container. After the initial sizzle, quickly cover the pot, sealing any gaps with kitchen towels to trap the smoke inside. Leave the pot undisturbed for 15 minutes.

Uncover the pot and remove the ghee container. (Alternatively, to dazzle your guests, take the entire pot to the table and remove the lid in front of them, letting the smoke billow out.) Sprinkle the fried shallots over the dish and serve warm with the sauce.

THE DHUNGAR METHOD

Outdoor cooking over charcoal or wood isn't the only way to infuse food with a smoky flavor. An age-old technique known as *dhungar* in India is also used in Southeast Asia, primarily within the Muslim community. Most often it is used to introduce a buttery, smoky flavor as a finishing touch to an already fully cooked dish.

The method involves an encounter between ghee (clarified butter), which is commonly used in South Asian cooking, and one or two hot coals. You can put the coals in a heatproof bowl and pour the ghee over them, or you can put the ghee in a heatproof bowl and add the coals to the ghee. Either way, there will be some sizzling followed by a white plume of smoke — savory, buttery, delicious — that you trap inside the smoking chamber. The chamber is typically a heavy, tightly covered pot of food with the small bowl holding the coals and ghee resting directly on whatever is being cooked, which can be anything from rice to *dal* to meats. Some cooks throw spices, such as cardamom pods, into the ghee along with the hot coals. Others hollow out an onion to look like a cup and use it in place of the bowl. But the basic concept is the same.

According to Harold McGee, food scientist and author of *On Food and Cooking: The Science and Lore of the Kitchen*, what happens in that small smoking chamber is similar to what happens in your backyard grill or smoker. In the case of the latter, you get smoke from anything in the food that showers down onto the burning coals, such as fat, sugar, and protein, in varying amounts. The *dhungar* method, in contrast, represents a much more controlled smoking environment in which you infuse food with the specific aroma derived from using the intense heat of a glowing piece of coal to transform the molecules of the ghee.

You can apply this method to various dishes, even those that don't come out of the South Asian culinary tradition. In winter when I don't feel like grilling food outdoors, I often cook many of the recipes in this book in the oven and then smoke them using the *dhungar* method. Barbecued Pork (page 125), for example, can be cooked in a home oven and then infused with smoky ghee.

CITRUS GRILLED CHICKEN
with Garlic Rice and Pickled Green Papaya

PICKLED GREEN PAPAYA

1 green papaya, about 1½ pounds

½ cup salt

4 ounces carrots

1 large red bell pepper

Thumb-size piece fresh ginger

1 small red onion

2 cups distilled white vinegar

1¼ cups granulated sugar

CHICKEN

4 large bone-in, skin-on chicken leg quarters (thigh and drumstick)

1 lemongrass stalk

4 large garlic cloves

1-inch piece fresh ginger, peeled and coarsely chopped

¼ cup coconut, unseasoned rice, or cider vinegar

½ cup fresh calamansi juice (see Note) or lime juice, or ¼ cup each fresh orange and lime juices

¼ cup packed light brown sugar

1 tablespoon salt

1 teaspoon freshly ground black pepper

BASTING LIQUID

½ cup vegetable oil

¼ cup unsalted butter or coconut oil, melted

2 tablespoons annatto seeds (see Note)

Marinated in fragrant coconut vinegar and calamansi juice and then generously brushed with annatto-infused oil as it cooks on the grill, *inasal na manok* is the iconic grilled chicken of Bacolod, a prosperous city on northwest coast of Negros Island in the Philippines. I like to serve this flavorful, colorful chicken with Filipino garlic fried rice (*sinangag*) and sweet and vinegary pickled green papaya (*atsarang papaya*) on the side.

Make the pickled green papaya in advance, as it tastes best after a couple of days in the refrigerator. Be sure to get your green papaya from an Asian store and pick one that is rock hard—so hard that it doesn't give at all when pressed against firmly with your thumb. You will need to grate the papaya, unless you are lucky enough to live near a well-stocked Southeast Asian market that carries pregrated green papaya in the refrigerated section—a great time-saver.

SERVES 4

To make the pickled papaya: Using a sharp paring knife or vegetable peeler, peel the papaya. Then, using a julienne hand grater, grate the flesh into thin 3- to 4-inch-long strands, stopping just before you get to the seeds. Transfer the strands to a large bowl. Reserve 2 tablespoons of the salt and mix the remaining salt into the papaya. Let stand for 1 hour.

Thoroughly rinse the salt off the papaya strands under cold running water, then rinse the bowl well. Squeeze the papaya dry with your hands and return it to the bowl. Peel the carrots, then grate them directly into the papaya bowl. Stem and seed the bell pepper, cut it lengthwise into ⅛-inch-wide strips, and add the strips to the papaya bowl. Peel the ginger, cut it into thin matchsticks, and add them to the papaya bowl. Peel the onion, halve it lengthwise, and cut each half lengthwise into ⅛-inch-thick slices. Add the slices to the bowl.

In a small saucepan, combine the vinegar, granulated sugar, and the reserved 2 tablespoons salt and bring to a boil over medium heat, stirring to dissolve the sugar and salt. Remove from the heat, pour it over the vegetables in the bowl, and stir well. Pack everything into a large glass jar or other container, cap tightly, and refrigerate for at least 2 days before serving. (This recipe makes more than you'll need for your meal, but the pickled papaya will keep refrigerated for 2 weeks.)

To prep the chicken: Put the chicken into a large bowl. Trim off the tough outer leaves and the root end from the lemongrass stalk. Beginning from the root end, use a very sharp knife to cut the bulb into thin slices, stopping when the purple rings disappear. In a blender, combine the lemongrass, garlic, ginger, vinegar, calamansi juice, brown sugar, salt, and pepper and blend to a smooth paste. Add the paste to the chicken and mix to coat the chicken evenly. Cover and refrigerate overnight.

The next day, make the basting liquid: In a small frying pan, combine the oil, butter, and annatto seeds over medium heat. When the fats starts to sizzle, after 1 to 2 minutes, remove the pan from the heat and leave the mixture to steep. Once it has cooled, strain through a fine-mesh sieve set over a small bowl and discard the solids. Set the liquid aside for basting the chicken.

Just before grilling the chicken, make the garlic rice: In a large wok or frying pan, combine the oil and garlic over medium heat and fry the garlic, stirring constantly, until golden brown, 5 to 7 minutes. Immediately remove the pan from the heat to stop the garlic from cooking further and burning. Stir the rice into the garlic and oil, add the salt, and mix well. Keep warm.

Prepare a medium-high fire (400° to 450°F) in a charcoal grill using the two-zone method (see page 11). When the coals are covered with white ash and the grate is hot, grill the chicken pieces, moving them back and forth between the hold side and the hot side and turning them frequently. Along the way, brush them with the prepared basting liquid, being careful of flare-ups. The chicken pieces are ready when they are golden brown and the internal temperature in the thickest part of a thigh away from bone registers 160°F, 40 to 45 minutes. Transfer the chicken to a platter and let rest for 10 minutes.

Serve with the garlic rice and some of the pickled papaya (keep the remainder refrigerated for future use).

GARLIC RICE

¼ cup vegetable oil

6 large garlic cloves, minced

4 cups cooked long-grain rice, separated into individual grains

½ teaspoon salt

NOTES >——————

Small, round, sharply sour calamansi citrus, also known as calamondin, a cross between orange and kumquat, can be hard to find in most areas of the United States. If you cannot source them, lime juice or a combination of orange and lime juice is an acceptable substitute.

Annatto seeds are the seeds from the achiote tree. The seeds are used to lend a deep orange-red color as well as their mildly earthy flavor to food. They can be found at any Latin market and many Asian markets.

GRILL-CHARRED BRAISED CHICKEN THIGHS

A classic of the Indonesian kitchen, *ayam panggang bumbu kecap* gives you the best of both worlds: bone-in chicken pieces braised in herbs and spices on the stove top until tender and finished on the grill to get both the skin—the best part—and the aromatics that cling to it smoky and charred. I'm using chicken thighs here because I find they remain juicy in twice-cooked dishes like this one.

SERVES 4

In a small food processor, blend the shallots, garlic, galangal, and coriander seeds to a smooth paste. Transfer the paste to a large Dutch oven, add ¼ cup of the kecap manis, 1½ teaspoons of the salt, the sugar, bay leaves, and lime leaves (if using), and stir well. Add the chicken thighs and just enough water to barely cover the ingredients.

Place the pot over medium-high heat and bring to a boil. Lower the heat to a gentle simmer and cook uncovered, replenishing the water as needed to keep it just covering the ingredients and restoring the simmer along the way, until the thighs are fork-tender but still hold their shape, 30 to 40 minutes, depending on their size. Turn off the heat and, using tongs, transfer the thighs, skin side up, to a sheet pan, being careful not to tear the skin or the meat. Let cool.

Prepare a medium-high fire (400° to 450°F) in a charcoal grill using the two-zone method (see page 11).

While the coals are heating, strain the cooking liquid through a fine-mesh sieve and discard the liquid. Transfer the solids in the sieve to a medium bowl and remove and discard the bay leaves. Stir in the remaining ¼ cup kecap manis, the remaining ½ teaspoon salt, and the oil. Use this mixture as the basting sauce.

When the coals are covered with white ash and the grate is hot, carefully arrange the chicken thighs, skin side down, in the center of the grill close to the hot side. Cook the thighs with the lid off, moving them back and forth between the hold side and the hot side of the grill and brushing them along the way with the basting sauce. The goal is to heat them through, char the skin, and crisp the basting mixture, which should take between 7 and 10 minutes.

Once that's done, transfer the thighs to a platter and arrange the lime wedges around them. Serve with the coconut rice and sambal.

2 ounces shallots, cubed

5 large garlic cloves

2 tablespoons chopped fresh galangal (see Note, page 102)

1 tablespoon coriander seeds

½ cup kecap manis (see Note)

2 teaspoons salt

¼ cup packed grated palm sugar or granulated coconut sugar, or 3 tablespoons packed light brown sugar

3 fresh bay leaves, or 2 dried bay leaves

2 makrut lime leaves (optional)

8 large bone-in, skin-on chicken thighs

½ cup vegetable oil

Lime wedges, for serving

Coconut rice (see page 51) or plain cooked jasmine rice, for serving

Sambal oelek (see page 52), for serving

NOTE

Kecap manis, a sweet dark soy sauce widely used in Indonesia as both a seasoning ingredient and a condiment or table sauce, can be difficult to find in the United States. Thai or Chinese sweet dark soy sauce is more routinely stocked at Asian grocery stores and makes a great substitute.

GRILLED STUFFED CHICKEN WINGS

CHICKEN

1 ounce dried glass noodles

2 teaspoons coconut oil

4 ounces white button mushrooms, finely chopped

4 ounces ground pork

2 tablespoons oyster sauce

1 tablespoon fish sauce

3 large garlic cloves, minced

2 tablespoons finely chopped fresh cilantro leaves and stems

1 teaspoon ground white or black pepper

16 large chicken wings

GLAZE

2 tablespoons soy sauce

1 tablespoon honey

1 teaspoon ground white or black pepper

¼ cup coconut oil, melted, or vegetable oil

Called "angel wings" at most Thai restaurants in the States, this dish has been a favorite among Southeast Asian immigrants in North America and Europe. Curiously, however, it's rarely served in Thailand. The restaurant version is deep-fried, but I've always cooked these wings on the grill. They taste better this way, and they hark back to the more rustic version made with frogs, which is well loved in rural areas in Cambodia, Thailand, and Laos.

The most challenging part of the recipe is the removal of the wing bones. If this is your first time, buy a few extra wings as practice pieces. It should take no more than three or four wings to get you in the groove. Then you'll whizz through the wings you need here in a matter of minutes. The recipe intentionally yields more stuffing than you need because it's nearly impossible to be precise unless the wings are all exactly the same size to start and therefore have the same capacity once they are boned. It's better to have too much than too little on hand. Besides, you can stir-fry what's left over and have yourself a snack portion of stir-fried glass noodles.

Glass noodles, also called bean thread noodles, are made of mung bean starch. Once cooked, they become translucent and slightly chewy, adding a nice texture to this dish. Choose a brand that is made from 100 percent mung bean starch, with no potato starch mixed in. Kaset is my favorite brand.

SERVES 4 AS AN APPETIZER

To stuff the chicken wings: In a medium bowl, soak the noodles in warm water to cover until softened, about 15 minutes. Drain, squeeze dry, and cut into ½-inch lengths. Return the noodles to the bowl.

Line a small plate with a paper towel. In a small frying pan, heat the coconut oil over medium-high heat. When the oil is hot, add the mushrooms and sauté until they turn soft and release some moisture, about 2 minutes. Using a slotted spoon, transfer the mushrooms to the towel-lined plate and let the paper towel absorb all the moisture. Transfer the mushrooms to the noodle bowl and add the pork, oyster sauce, fish sauce, garlic, cilantro, and pepper. Mix until well blended and sticky, then cover and refrigerate.

Take a chicken wing and cut through the joint connecting the drumette with the rest of the wing. Reserve the drumette for another use and put the partial wing—the wingette and wing tip—into a large bowl. Repeat with the remaining wings.

>> CONTINUED

Take a partial wing and use your hands to break it in two at the joint where the wingette meets the tip, without breaking through the skin. Using the tip of a very sharp paring knife, make a cut around the very top part where the meat is attached to the joint bone. Carefully pull down the wingette meat toward the wing tip to expose the bones that run through the wingette, inserting your finger inside the wingette to help loosen things up. Pull those bones out while keeping the meat, skin, and shape of the wingette intact; discard the bones. Repeat with the remaining partial wings. Now you have sixteen boned wings with empty pockets ready to be filled.

Stuff the wings with the pork mixture and close each opening with a wooden toothpick. Put in as much of the stuffing as you can to create full pockets, but don't overfill, as the filling will expand a little during cooking.

Bring water in a steamer bottom to a gentle boil. Arrange the wings in a single layer in a steamer container, place over (not touching) the gently boiling water, cover, and steam until the juices run clear when a wing is tested with a knife tip, about 10 minutes. Remove the wings from the steamer, blot them dry, and leave them to cool on a sheet pan. Don't remove the toothpicks just yet.

Prepare a medium-high fire (400° to 450°F) in a charcoal grill using the two-zone method (see page 11).

Meanwhile, make the glaze: In a small bowl, whisk together the soy sauce, honey, pepper, and oil.

When the coals are covered with white ash and the grate is hot, place the wings on the hold side of the grill, cover, and cook with the vents fully opened, removing the lid and brushing the wings with the glaze along the way. The wings are already fully cooked, so at this point you only need to grill them just until they're heated through and golden brown, which should take anywhere between 10 and 12 minutes.

Transfer the wings to a platter, remove the toothpicks, leave them to cool to slightly warmer than room temperature, and serve.

USING BANANA LEAVES TO GRILL

Southeast Asian cooks have used edible plants as cooking vessels since ancient times. Bamboo stalks, for example, are used throughout the region to cook everything from rice to braised meats. Coconut shell halves work well, too. The leaves of a plant, however, are used more than any other part for cooking. Palm leaves, lotus leaves, and taro leaves are among the most typical. But no leaf is more frequently used and more deeply ingrained in the everyday cooking than the banana leaf.

Banana leaves are common — most homes have banana trees — affordable, and easy to work with. They are flexible yet strong, don't disintegrate when boiled, can withstand the heat from an open fire, and lend their tea-like scent to whatever food comes in contact with them. In the United States, they are almost always sold frozen. This is actually not a bad thing when it comes to grilling. I've found that once frozen and thawed, the leaves don't burn as easily and are less likely to tear than fresh leaves. You need to be sure to thaw them completely, however, as they are prone to breaking if used frozen or semifrozen.

Preparing banana leaves for cooking is very easy once you get a feel for it. They usually come in pieces 8 to 12 inches wide of various lengths, often in 1-pound packages. The leaves vary in thickness and strength. More mature banana leaves are thicker and stronger than younger ones. The area of the banana tree the pieces come from matters, too. Pieces taken from the base are thicker and stronger than those taken from near the tip of the leaf, which tend to be thin and fragile. The leaves in a single package aren't uniform, which means you'll have to use your judgment sometimes. If the square you're working with seems too thin to hold the food securely throughout the cooking process, use a double layer. In that case, make sure the grain of one piece runs perpendicular to the grain of the second piece to create a stronger packet. Leftover thawed banana leaves can be loosely folded, deposited into a gallon-size ziptop bag, and refrozen for later use.

Use wooden toothpicks to secure the seams or folds, and make sure the toothpicks are perpendicular to the grain of the leaves.

GRILLED SOY SAUCE CHICKEN WINGS

Watching a grill master cook these Malaysian-style chicken wings is mesmerizing. I can't tell you how many times I have declared that I am famished and ready to eat, approached a chicken wings stall at a *pasar malam* (night market), and then was unable to leave the action at the grill and find a seat.

Imagine a trident—the kind the Greek god Poseidon uses to stir up tidal waves and sea storms when he's bored and cranky—but with its handle very short and its three prongs very long. That's the three-pronged spit that Malaysian vendors use to prepare their famous wings, a cult favorite in the southern part of mainland Southeast Asia.

The vendor places the tridents loaded with wings a few inches from the flaming coals and, while keeping a close watch on the fire, spins the handle of each trident almost constantly to ensure even cooking. We're talking about a manual rotisserie that spins nearly as fast as a top, accompanied by the hissing of rendered chicken fat hitting the burning coals. After a few moments of spellbinding spinning (with an occasional pause for basting), the wings have become smoky and have taken on the color of dark amber and their skin is nearly as crisp as chips.

We home cooks aren't equipped with that kind of grilling equipment or armed with years of experience spinning a rotisserie over hot coals. So when I make these wings at home, I have to get creative. After many experiments, I've settled on cooking the wings at a low temperature in my pellet smoker, using either pecan or hickory wood for fuel, until they're smoky and golden brown. At that point, the skin has rendered some of its fat and is somewhat dry. That's when the wings are perfectly primed for the final finishing touch of high-heat cooking, which crisps and chars the skin.

2 thumb-size pieces fresh ginger, cubed

2 ounces shallots, cubed

6 large garlic cloves

2 tablespoons water

1 teaspoon salt

3 tablespoons honey

2 tablespoons soy sauce

2 tablespoons oyster sauce

2 tablespoons vegetable oil

2 teaspoons toasted sesame oil

1 teaspoon ground white or black pepper

12 chicken wings

American Sriracha (such as Huy Fong brand, aka "rooster sauce") or other chile sauce, for serving (optional)

Lime wedges, for serving

Cilantro springs, for serving

SERVES 4 AS AN APPETIZER

In a blender, combine the ginger, shallots, garlic, water, and salt and blend until smooth. Strain the mixture through a fine-mesh sieve set over a large bowl, using the back of a spoon to press through as much liquid as possible; discard the solids. Add the honey, soy sauce, oyster sauce, both oils, and the pepper and mix well. Add the wings and stir to coat evenly. Cover and refrigerate overnight.

Heat a smoker to 225°F. Smoke the wings until the internal temperature registers 160°F, about 2 hours. Increase the heat of the smoker to 400°F and grill the wings until crisp, 5 to 7 minutes.

Transfer the wings to a platter and leave to cool for 15 minutes, then serve with the chile sauce, if desired, and the lime wedges and cilantro.

COCONUT-TURMERIC GRILLED CHICKEN

6 large garlic cloves

3 cilantro roots, chopped, or 3 tablespoons finely chopped fresh cilantro stems stripped of leaves

¼ cup fish sauce

¼ cup packed grated palm sugar or granulated coconut sugar, or 3 tablespoons packed light brown sugar

½ cup unsweetened full-fat coconut milk

2 whole chickens, 3½ to 4 pounds each, halved with the spine either removed or attached to one of the halves

½ cup coconut oil

2 tablespoons ground turmeric

2 tablespoons coriander seeds, coarsely ground in a mortar or spice grinder

1 tablespoon white or black peppercorns, coarsely ground

The grilled chicken of the village of Bang Tan, in the southwest corner of central Thailand, is another prominent member of the Thai grilled chicken pantheon. It's casually referred to as "train station chicken" or "train chicken" because it's sold by the many hawkers who flood every train that stops at the Bang Tan station on its way toward—or back from—the south.

Kai yang bang tan has its own unique appearance, which you can spot from afar. Chicken quarters are partially boned, then flattened, stretched taut between bamboo wood that has been split into three prongs—the chicken's signature look—and secured with strings made from the dried stems of water hyacinths. The chicken, which has a yellow tint from the turmeric in the marinade, is grilled and smoked over low coals until the exterior is dry to the touch. And this is what makes Bang Tan grilled chicken special: it looks dry and devoid of any fatty juices, but it's actually juicy and smoky.

I have several versions of Bang Tan–inspired grilled chicken in my repertoire, but in recent years, I have become smitten with this one, which involves smoking the chicken halves in a barrel cooker (see page 6) until the meat is barely cooked through but the skin is dry from rendering its fat during the cooking process. Alternatively, you can smoke the chicken in a kettle grill following the instructions on page 4 or in a pellet grill/smoker (see page 6). At this stage, the skin will have a rubbery texture, so I sear the smoked chicken briefly on a hot grill to crisp it up. The result is impossibly juicy meat with crisp, charred skin.

SERVES 4 TO 6

In a small processor, combine the garlic, cilantro roots, fish sauce, sugar, and coconut milk and blend until smooth. Rub the mixture all over the chicken halves—on the bone side, on the skin, and under the wings—then put the chicken into a large bowl. Cover and refrigerate overnight.

About 1 hour before you begin to cook the chicken, heat the oil in a small frying pan over medium heat just until warm. Remove from the heat and stir in the turmeric. Set aside to cool.

Prepare a barrel cooker for smoking according to the manufacturer's instructions.

Take the chicken out of the refrigerator and wipe the marinade off the skin with damp paper towels. Leave the bone side as is. Pat the skin dry. Brush the skin thoroughly with half of the turmeric oil and sprinkle the coriander and pepper all over the skin, pressing down lightly to help the spices adhere.

Hang the chicken halves inside the cooker over the coals and cook with the vents open about ½ inch until the internal temperature at the thigh registers 140°F, about 2 hours. Toward the end of the cooking time, prepare a medium-high fire (400° to 450°F) in a charcoal grill using the two-zone method (see page 11).

Transfer the chicken, skin side up, to a sheet pan. Brush the skin evenly and thoroughly with the remaining turmeric oil. When the coals are covered with white ash and the grate is hot, place the chicken, skin side up, in the center of the grill between the hot side and the hold side. Cook, covered and with the vents fully opened, until the internal temperature in the thickest part of the thigh registers 155°F, 5 to 7 minutes. Turn the chicken skin side down on the hot side of the grill and cook, covered and with the vents fully closed, until the internal temperature at the thigh reaches 160°F and the skin side is crisp and lightly charred all over, about 10 minutes longer.

(If using a pellet grill/smoker, set the temperature at 225°F. Place the chicken halves, skin side up, on the grate and cook, covered, until the internal temperature at the thigh registers 140°F, about 1 hour and 15 minutes. Brush the chicken with the remaining turmeric oil and increase the temperature to 425°F. Cook until the internal temperature at the thigh reaches 160°F and the skin side is crisp and lightly charred all over, about 15 minutes longer.)

Transfer the chicken to a cutting board and leave to rest for 20 minutes. Carve and serve.

MADURA CHICKEN SATAY

with Easy Rice Cakes

CHICKEN

2 tablespoons fresh lime juice

½ teaspoon salt

3 large garlic cloves, pressed or minced

1 teaspoon ground white or black pepper

1½ pounds boneless, skinless chicken thighs, cut into ½-inch dice

PEANUT SAUCE

2 large dried Thai long chiles or guajillo chiles, cut into 1-inch pieces

2 lemongrass stalks

1 ounce shallots, cubed

2 large garlic cloves

2 tablespoons vegetable oil

¾ cup ground unsalted roasted peanuts

¾ cup water

1 tablespoon kecap manis (see Note, page 81)

1 tablespoon packed light brown sugar

½ teaspoon salt

CRISPY SHALLOTS

½ cup paper-thin shallot slices

¾ cup vegetable oil

RICE CAKES

2 cups freshly cooked jasmine rice, kept warm

FOR SERVING

2 limes, cut into wedges

Thinly sliced shallots

Thinly sliced fresh hot chiles

Coarsely chopped cucumber

There are too many types of satay (*sate* in Indonesian) to list them all, says Pat Tanumihardja, food writer and expert on Indonesian cuisine. Chicken, beef, lamb, and pork varieties are common, of course, as are ones made with organ meats. However, less common meats, such as rabbit and duck, are also found in the satay realm, says Tanumihardja, who adores chicken skin satay but doesn't feel the same way about *sate torpedo*, made with lamb testicles, which she was tricked into eating as a young child.

The sauces that accompany satay vary, too. The two best known are the standard peanut sauce, which is found all over Indonesia, with the Javanese version being a tad sweeter than most, and one made with *kecap manis* (sweet dark soy sauce), shallots, and bird's eye chiles that is just as loved. But there are others, Tanumihardja points out, citing as one of the many examples a lesser-known iteration from West Sumatra, a smooth, velvety peanut sauce perfumed with turmeric and thickened with rice flour and/or tapioca starch.

While thick-cut toast is the de rigueur starch in a satay meal in Thailand, in Singapore and Malaysia, *ketupat*, plain boiled rice dumplings wrapped in woven palm leaves, are typical. In Indonesia, *lontong*, cylindrical rice cakes wrapped in banana leaves and cut into disks, are a familiar face at any satay table, she says.

This recipe, *sate ayam madura*, is from Madura, an island off the coast of Java. The chicken is cut into small dice and paired with peanut sauce with some *kecap manis* added to it. The satay is typically served drenched in the sauce and topped with crispy fried shallots. Lime wedges, cucumber chunks, chopped fresh chiles, and fresh shallot slices are arranged to one side of the plate. I've also included a shortcut for making an approximation of rice cakes, or *lontong*. Serve them along with the satay.

———————————————————————————⟨ SERVES 4 AS AN APPETIZER

To prep the chicken: In a large bowl, combine the lime juice, salt, garlic, and pepper and mix well. Add the chicken and stir to coat evenly. Cover and refrigerate for 2 hours. Soak sixteen 12-inch bamboo skewers in water to cover for 1 to 2 hours.

>> CONTINUED

To make the peanut sauce: In a small bowl, combine the chiles with warm water to cover and let stand until softened, about 15 minutes. Squeeze the pieces dry and add to a small food processor. Trim off the tough outer leaves and the root end of each lemongrass stalk. Beginning from the root end, use a very sharp knife to cut each bulb into thin slices, stopping when the purple rings disappear. Add the lemongrass to the processor along with the shallots and garlic and process to a smooth paste.

Scrape the paste into a 1-quart saucepan and add the oil. Set over medium heat and fry until the paste is fragrant, 1 to 2 minutes. Stir in the peanuts, water, kecap manis, sugar, and salt and simmer for 2 minutes. Taste and adjust the seasoning if needed, aiming for sweet and salty. The sauce should be pourable, so if it's too thick, whisk in more water as needed. Set aside ¼ cup of the sauce; keep the remaining sauce warm in the pan.

To make the crispy shallots: Set a fine-mesh sieve over a small heatproof bowl and put it near the stove. In a small frying pan, combine the shallots and oil over medium-low heat and heat slowly, stirring occasionally. When the shallots begin to sizzle, start stirring more frequently so they cook evenly (the pieces around the edge of the pan will brown first). When the shallots are golden brown, after about 7 minutes, promptly pour the contents of the pan into the sieve. Leave the fried shallots in the sieve; reserve the oil for another use.

To shape the rice cakes: Spoon the rice onto the center of a large piece of parchment paper. Using the paper as an aid, shape the rice into a compact log about 1 inch in diameter, with no gaps among the grains. Roll up the log in the parchment, twist the ends tightly closed, and keep warm.

Take the chicken out of the refrigerator. Stir in the reserved ¼ cup peanut sauce. Thread the chicken onto the soaked skewers (see opposite page).

Light a full chimney of charcoal. When the coals are ready, spread them out on the bottom of a hibachi (preferable) or kettle grill for cooking over high fire.

When the coals are covered with white ash and the grate is hot, grill the chicken, turning often, until cooked through and lightly charred, about 10 minutes.

Arrange the satay on a platter. Check on the reserved peanut sauce; if it has thickened on sitting, whisk in enough water to make it pourable and heat through. Pour the sauce on top of the satay. Sprinkle the crispy shallots over the sauce. Arrange the limes, fresh shallots, chiles, and cucumber on the platter. Unwrap the rice log, cut it into 1-inch-thick slices, and arrange the slices on a separate plate to serve on the side. Enjoy immediately.

HOW TO THREAD MEAT ONTO A SKEWER

One of the things that has always annoyed and amused me in equal measure is the way "Asian skewers" are pictured in mainstream food publications or on websites: a single long, narrow piece of meat is threaded onto a bamboo skewer, stretched taut. The meat department of a certain big-box store has prepackaged, ready-to-cook meat labeled "Asian-style BBQ beef skewers" that fits that description. The way it looks is as cringe-worthy as the label.

Aside from the fact that's not how it's usually done in Asia, it's impractical. When a single piece of meat is threaded onto a bamboo skewer in an up-and-down sewing fashion, bad things happen. The skewer will be exposed directly to the fire during grilling, and even if the skewer was soaked, it will likely burn. Also, when meat comes served in one piece like this, you have to either tear the meat at its midpoint with your front teeth or eat the whole piece in one bite. Neither makes for a pleasant experience. When meat is threaded onto a skewer in this manner, it is more prone to drying out as well. And things get much worse if the meat has also been cut with the grain.

The antidote to this single-long-piece problem is to cut the meat into bite-size pieces, which minimizes the length of the muscle fiber, making it easier to eat. Thread the pieces onto a skewer, packing them somewhat tightly against one another. This helps keep the meat moist and prevents the bamboo skewers from being exposed to the fire. And when it's time to eat, you can conveniently enjoy one bite's worth of meat at a time.

GRILLED CHICKEN SKEWERS

with Sweet-and-Sour Curry Sauce

15 large dried Thai long chiles or guajillo chiles, cut into 1-inch pieces

4-inch piece fresh ginger, diced

10 large garlic cloves

2 teaspoons ground coriander

2 teaspoons ground cinnamon

4-inch piece fresh turmeric root, diced, or 1 tablespoon ground turmeric

1 ounce shallots, diced

5 pounds boneless, skin-on chicken thighs, or 7 pounds bone-in, skin-on chicken thighs, boned

6 cups unsweetened full-fat coconut milk

5 teaspoons salt

¼ cup coconut or vegetable oil

1 cup packed grated Thai palm sugar or granulated coconut sugar, or ⅔ cup packed light brown sugar

¼ cup tamarind paste (see Note, page 23)

Cilantro leaves, for garnish

Coconut rice (see page 51) or plain cooked jasmine rice, for serving

Hailing from the deep south of Thailand, where the influences of Muslim cooking are most prominent, this lesser-known classic grilled chicken, called *kai yang kolae*, is in a category of its own—completely different from its better-known grilled counterpart in the northeast in terms of both flavor and presentation. It is marinated in a spice paste that also serves as the base for a sauce used for both basting and serving.

I recommend that you keep the skin on the chicken. When the basting sauce and the chicken fat in the skin fall onto the coals, a wonderfully fragrant smoke rises up to perfume the meat. This is part of what makes this dish so well loved.

SERVES 8

In a small bowl, combine the chiles with warm water to cover and let stand until softened, about 15 minutes. Squeeze the pieces dry and add to a small food processor along with the ginger, garlic, coriander, cinnamon, turmeric, and shallots. Process to a smooth paste.

Cut the chicken into 2-inch cubes and put them into a large bowl. Add half of the prepared paste, 1 cup of the coconut milk, and 2 teaspoons of the salt and mix well. Cover and refrigerate for 6 to 8 hours. Put the remaining curry paste in a covered container and the remaining 5 cups coconut milk in a separate container. Refrigerate until needed.

In a 2-quart saucepan, combine the remaining curry paste and the oil, set over medium heat, and fry until the paste is fragrant, about 2 minutes. Stir in the remaining 5 cups coconut milk, the remaining 3 teaspoons salt, the sugar, and tamarind. Bring the sauce to a gentle boil, lower the heat, and simmer, stirring often, for 3 minutes. Remove from the heat. Split the sauce into two equal portions. Use one portion to baste the chicken and reserve the second portion for drizzling over the chicken once it's cooked.

Prepare a medium-high fire (400° to 450°F) in a charcoal grill using the two-zone method (see page 11).

Thread the chicken onto metal skewers. When the coals are covered with white ash and the grate is hot, place the chicken on the hold side of the grill. Cover and cook with the vents half-opened, brushing with the basting sauce and turning every 5 minutes. When the chicken is almost entirely opaque, after about 15 minutes, move the skewers closer to the hot side of the grill and, watching carefully, cook until the chicken is charred, 7 to 10 minutes. Transfer to a platter, tent with aluminum foil, and let rest for 15 minutes.

Warm up the reserved sauce for serving and drizzle it over the chicken. Garnish the chicken with cilantro and serve immediately with the rice.

HONEY-ROASTED DUCK

with Pickled Ginger and Chile-Soy-Vinegar Sauce

In the United States, we're accustomed to the Cantonese-style roasted ducks offered in Chinatowns around the country. In Thailand, ducks cooked Cantonese-style—or Hong Kong–style, as the Thais say—can be found, too. But it's the roasted ducks made in the tradition of the Teochew diaspora that dominate the scene.

An observant eater will notice a few differences: Teochew roasted ducks in Thailand sport tender, charred skin, while their Cantonese counterparts have crispier, glossier skin. In terms of taste, Teochew Thai cooks subtly infuse the duck with local Thai herbs—lemongrass, galangal, makrut lime leaves—something that's not done in Cantonese roasted ducks. Another subtle difference is the tendency of Teochew cooks in Thailand to favor fermented soybean paste over hoisin sauce, which permeates Cantonese barbecue. The fermented soybean paste—aka salted soybean paste or sauce, or *tao-jiao*—is a thick, umami-packed seasoning. In a pinch, dark miso can be substituted in the recipes in this book.

Read through the recipe carefully before you begin so you can plan for it. It isn't difficult, but it extends over two days. This is, therefore, not a weeknight meal, but instead a fun weekend project.

SERVES 4 GENEROUSLY

Trim four bamboo skewers to 4 inches from the pointed end and set aside.

To make the sauce: In a small glass jar, combine the vinegar, soy sauce, and honey and stir until well blended. Add the chile slices. Cover and refrigerate for 2 days.

Right after you're done with the sauce, prep the duck: In a blender, combine the garlic, ginger, cilantro root, five-spice powder, oyster sauce, salt, 2 tablespoons of the soy sauce, the fermented soybean paste, ¼ cup of the honey, and the wine and process until smooth. Remove the wing tips and pat the duck dry. Stretch the skin flap at the neck to cover the neck hole and secure it with one of the bamboo skewers. With one hand grabbing the duck by its two legs, hold the duck head end down and pour the marinade into the cavity, rubbing it all over while keeping the skin on the outside dry and clean. Fill the cavity with the lemongrass and galangal and lime leaves, if using. Pull the skin flaps over the cavity and use the remaining skewers to "sew" the cavity shut (the goal is to keep the marinade inside). Wipe the skin clean of any wayward marinade.

>> CONTINUED

SAUCE

½ cup distilled white or cider vinegar

½ cup soy sauce

2 tablespoons honey

4 fresh green Thai long chiles or jalapeño or serrano peppers, sliced ¼ inch thick

DUCK

3 large garlic cloves

3 thin fresh ginger slices

2 tablespoons coarsely chopped cilantro roots or fresh cilantro stems stripped of leaves

2 tablespoons Chinese five-spice powder

2 tablespoons oyster sauce

1 teaspoon salt

2 tablespoons plus ½ cup soy sauce

¼ cup fermented soybean paste (see headnote) or miso

½ cup honey

1 tablespoon Shaoxing rice wine (see Note, page 126)

1 White Pekin duck, about 5 pounds, head removed

2 lemongrass stalks, each smashed to split the bulb, then tied into a knot

3 or 4 fresh galangal slices (optional; see Note, page 102)

3 or 4 makrut lime leaves, hand torn (optional)

12 cups water

¼ cup distilled white vinegar

PICKLED GINGER

4 ounces fresh ginger
(see Note)

1 teaspoon salt

2 tablespoons granulated
sugar

½ cup distilled white,
unseasoned rice, or cider
vinegar

1 tablespoon undiluted raw
beet juice, for color

GLAZE

¼ cup water

2 tablespoons soy sauce

2 tablespoons honey

1 teaspoon distilled white
vinegar

2 tablespoons vegetable oil,
for brushing

1 cup sliced cucumbers, for
serving

Cooked jasmine rice, for
serving

NOTE ›————————

If possible, use young fresh
ginger with thin, smooth
skin, often with a pink blush,
and tender flesh, rather than
mature ginger with brown,
papery skin and fibrous flesh.
It is most commonly seen in
the US at farmers' markets
in the spring.

Select a 4-quart saucepan that is wider that the circumference of the widest part of the duck. Add the water, the remaining ½ cup soy sauce, the remaining ¼ cup honey, and the vinegar to the pan and bring to a boil over high heat. Meanwhile, set a rack on a sheet pan and keep it nearby. With one hand, hold the duck firmly by the "ankles" a couple of inches above the boiling liquid; with the other hand, ladle the liquid over the duck. Do this repeatedly, scalding every square inch of the skin, for 2 minutes. Place the duck, breast side up, on the rack and refrigerate the duck on the sheet pan for 24 hours to marinate the inside and dry out the skin. Discard the liquid.

Meanwhile, make the pickled ginger: Cut the ginger crosswise on a sharp diagonal into paper-thin slices (use a mandoline if you have one). Mix ½ teaspoon of the salt into the ginger and let sit for 30 minutes. Rinse the ginger well, squeeze it dry, and place it in a clean glass jar. In a small saucepan, combine the sugar, vinegar, and the remaining ½ teaspoon salt over medium heat until the sugar and salt dissolve and the mixture is lukewarm. Remove from the heat and pour it over the ginger. Stir in the beet juice (the juice must be raw for staining power). Cap the jar and refrigerate until serving.

To make the glaze: In a small bowl, whisk together the water, soy sauce, honey, and vinegar. Keep covered at room temperature until roasting time.

Prepare a fire in a charcoal grill using the two-zone method (see page 11), keeping the temperature steady at 350°F. When the coals are covered with white ash and the grate is hot, place the duck on the hold side of the grill. Cover and roast, adjusting the vents to maintain the temperature and rotating and flipping the duck every 15 minutes, until the internal temperature taken at the thickest part of the thigh registers 150°F. This should take close to 2 hours. Brush the prepared glaze all over the duck, re-cover, and continue to cook until the internal temperature registers 160°F, about 20 minutes longer (watch the duck closely during this time as the skin can burn easily). Transfer the duck to a large rimmed platter and brush all over with the oil. Let rest for 45 minutes.

Remove and discard the bamboo skewers. Empty out the cavity into a small bowl, keeping the liquid and discarding the solids. Carve the duck and arrange it on a serving platter with the pickled ginger and cucumber slices. Drizzle the liquid from the cavity over the duck. Serve with the rice and a small bowl of the sauce on the side.

ROASTED DUCK IN BANANA LEAF PACKETS

2 large lemongrass stalks

2 ounces shallots, cubed

3 large garlic cloves

¼ cup diced fresh ginger

3 thin fresh galangal slices
(see Note, page 102)

2-inch piece fresh turmeric
root, sliced, or 1 tablespoon
ground turmeric

2 teaspoons white or black
peppercorns

1 tablespoon coriander seeds

2 teaspoons freshly grated
or ground nutmeg

6 to 8 fresh red bird eye's
chiles, sliced

2 tablespoons packed light
brown sugar

1 tablespoon salt

4 large duck leg quarters,
each about 1 pound

1 cup fresh basil leaves
(preferably lemon or Thai)

4 fresh or dried bay leaves

4 makrut lime leaves,
deveined and thinly sliced
(optional)

4 (14-inch) square pieces
banana leaf

Cooked jasmine rice,
for serving

I had my first exposure to Indonesian food in grade school when my mother's friend from Indonesia, Auntie Leslie, was staying with us during her short visit to Bangkok. She'd cook dinner for us, Auntie Leslie declared. It would be a roasted duck, she said, putting a whole duck she'd bought at the market in the fridge. With a cleaver in hand, Auntie Leslie asked me to follow her to our backyard with a basket and help her carry the things she needed to gather from our garden.

Her first target was one of our banana trees. She cut a large bunch of banana leaves, along with their stems. I had to drag those leaves—they were taller than I was—into the house, permanently staining my shirt with banana sap. Then she had me walk around our garden with her, digging up our ginger, galangal, and turmeric roots and picking a bucketful of lemon basil leaves—a basil variety used throughout Southeast Asia with a delicate citrus scent—and some chiles.

That dinner turned out to be *bebek betutu*, one of the specialties of her hometown in Bali. She marinated the duck in a spice paste, wrapped it in banana leaves, wrapped it again in the bark-like parts of the banana leaf stems (to keep the more delicate leaves from burning and disintegrating), and cooked it slowly over a charcoal fire until the meat was fairly tender and the fire had died down. This recipe follows Auntie Leslie's quite closely, but I use heavy-duty aluminum foil in place of the banana leaf stems, which would be impossible to get unless you have banana trees in your backyard. Before you begin, see page 85 for tips on purchasing and handling banana leaves.

⤙ SERVES 4

Trim off the tough outer leaves and the root end from each lemongrass stalk. Beginning from the root end, use a very sharp knife to cut each bulb into thin slices, stopping when the purple rings disappear. Transfer to a small food processor or a mortar and add the shallots, garlic, ginger, galangal, turmeric, peppercorns, coriander, nutmeg, chiles, sugar, and salt and grind to a smooth paste (in a food processor, add a little water if needed to get the blades going).

Put the duck into a large ziptop plastic bag. Add the marinade, press out the air, seal the bag closed, and turn and massage the bag to coat the duck with the marinade. Refrigerate for 1 hour.

>> CONTINUED

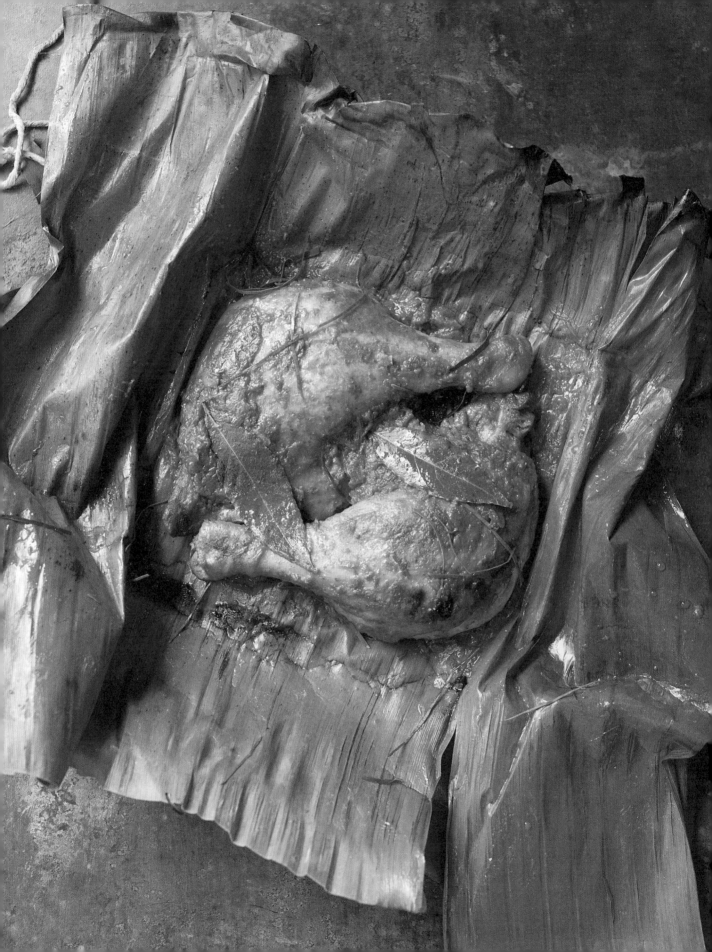

NOTE >————————————

Galangal, a member of the ginger family, is a rhizome with pale beige, glossy skin and a sharp, somewhat citrusy flavor. Sometimes labeled "Thai ginger" or "blue ginger," it is typically sliced and occasionally chopped and is usually displayed near darker beige, rougher-skinned ginger in the produce departments of Asian markets.

Prepare a medium fire in a charcoal grill using the two-zone method (see page 11), keeping the temperature steady at 350°F.

Meanwhile, cut four 18-inch squares of heavy-duty aluminum foil. Arrange the foil squares side by side on a work surface and center a banana leaf square on each foil square. Place ¼ cup of the basil leaves in the center of each banana leaf, followed by a duck leg quarter. Top with 1 bay leaf and the makrut lime leaf slices (if using). Fold up the sides of each foil square to form a tightly sealed packet.

Place the packets on the hold side of the grill, cover, and cook, adjusting the vents to maintain the temperature and turning the packets around every 15 minutes so they heat evenly from all sides, for 2 hours.

Remove the packets from the grill, open them up, and discard the bay leaves. Serve the duck in the packets, with the rice on the side.

TRANG-STYLE ROASTED SUCKLING PIG

A suckling pig, weighing between 25 and 28 pounds, completely thawed (if previously frozen) but ice cold (see Note, page 109)

2 cups soy sauce

¼ cup salt

2 heads garlic, peeled

1-inch piece ginger, peeled and roughly chopped

½ vegetable oil

¼ cup distilled white vinegar

¼ cup Chinese five-spice powder

1 tablespoon red pepper flakes, or more to taste

¾ cup Chinese black vinegar or apple cider vinegar

¼ cup packed dark brown sugar

To eat out at breakfast in the southern Thai province of Trang is to experience a small-scale feast—intimate, leisurely, plentiful. The table overflows with choices that tell the story of Chinese immigrants who crossed the water and landed there at the turn of the twentieth century—dim sum in bamboo baskets, rice porridge topped with cut-up crullers—as well as with such local fare as fermented rice noodles and fiery, turmeric-laced fish curry accompanied with a bounteous basket of leafy herbs, berries, and shoots.

Overshadowing all of these is the town's most renowned dish: *mu yang trang*, or "roasted pork in the style of Trang," a designation that confirms its uniqueness. It's an indispensable part of the Trang-style breakfast that locals enjoy with their morning cup of joe, giving a sideways stare to anyone who dares suggest it's an odd pairing.

The reason roasted pork is a breakfast item in Trang is because hogs are traditionally roasted there during the night. By the crack of dawn, the roasted pigs are ready to be cut into huge bone-in, skin-on chunks and delivered to local morning markets and old-school coffee shops, where customers have already lined up to get the choicest cuts. They know that at this time of day the meat is at its most succulent and the skin is still so crisp that it collapses into shards at first bite.

Roasting whole hogs, Trang-style, is a long, arduous process that is taken on exclusively by roasters who work around the clock preparing the pigs during the day and roasting them at night. The process begins with a young hog of 130 to 140 pounds—eviscerated, washed, and butterflied. With the hip bones and leg bones removed, the fleshy part below the rib cage is exposed. The meat side is scored in a tight diamond pattern, about an inch deep, before a spice rub—coconut sugar, salt, and fragrant dried spices—is applied liberally onto its every nook and cranny. The pig is then left to marinate for about 12 hours.

Once the coals are hot and the clay oven, built into the ground, is properly heated, the pig is attached to a large hook and secured with wooden dowels firmly placed across the breast and hip areas to keep the body spread open. The pig is then lowered headfirst into the pit for a quick round of roasting that lasts only 10 to 15 minutes—just long enough for the skin to contract and become taut. It is then pulled back up from the pit; its extremities are wrapped in aluminum foil to prevent burning; its skin is thoroughly pricked; and the whole thing is mopped with a mixture of diluted soy sauce, vinegar, and honey.

≫ CONTINUED

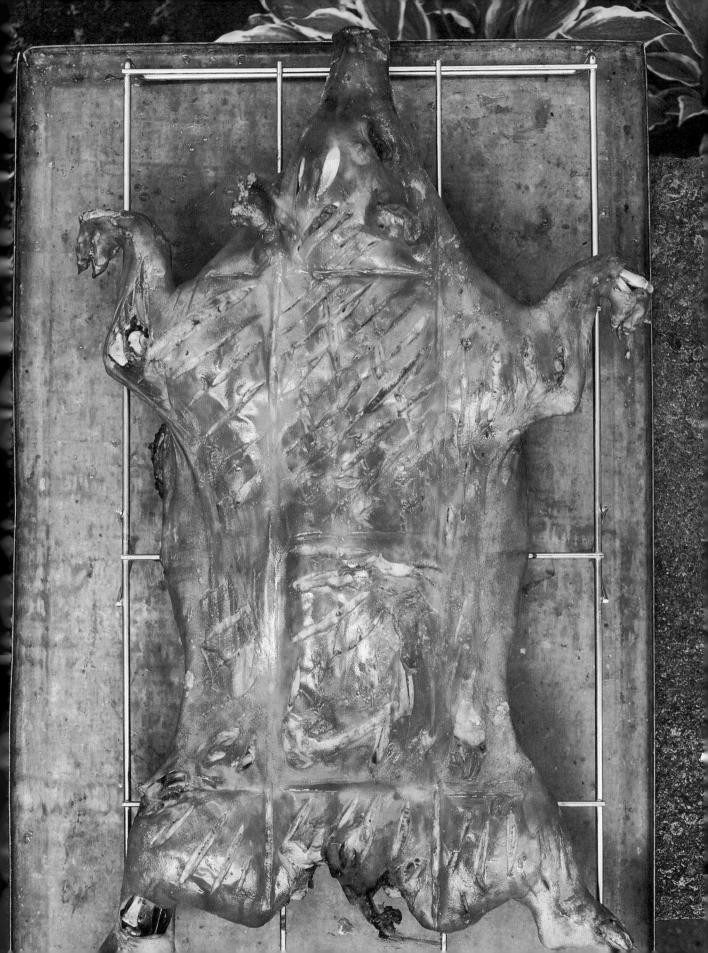

Finally, it's lowered back into the pit, where it remains until the meat is cooked through and the skin turns golden brown from snout to tail.

In the absence of the professional roasting equipment and the complex technique that veteran roasters in Trang spend decades perfecting, my adaptation serves home cooks better. You'll be cooking a suckling pig, which is very easy to handle, unlike a larger, older hog. Plus, its abundance of collagen makes the meat forgiving and likely to come out tender and succulent, even in the hands of an inexperienced roaster. Also, instead of digging a hole in your backyard and building an oven pit in the ground, you'll use a pig roasting box (see page 6), which is popular with hog-roasting enthusiasts who are home cooks.

This method has its disadvantages, however. One is a lack of control over the doneness, as you're not supposed to peek at the pig every few minutes, which would cause the temperature to fluctuate. When the marinade contains a lot of sugar—and that's the case with the traditional Trang-style roasted pigs—you risk burning your pig before it's cooked through. This is why I break with tradition here and introduce the sugar to the dish in the dipping sauce.

The other disadvantage is that the natural curvature of the back of the pig creates varying distances between it and the coals on the lid, resulting in unevenly crisped skin. I solve this problem by roasting the skin side of the pig just until the prominent parts are charred and crisp to my liking, then I take the pig out of the box and bring the undercrisped parts up to speed with a high-powered kitchen torch. You want the skin to be evenly browned, blistered, dotted with tiny little bubbles, and thoroughly crisp.

That said, a roasting box is convenient. Moving and flipping the pig is a two-person job, but because the box does most of the work, it makes a virtual trip to the south of Thailand a breeze. Too bad it doesn't also brew coffee for you to drink with your morning roasted pork.

————————————————————————————————< SERVES 12 TO 14

Lay the pig on its back and wipe the inside dry with paper towels. Using a heavy cleaver (in conjunction with a rubber mallet, if necessary), make a few cuts along the spine, being careful not to cut all the way through. Push down hard on both sides of the pig's body, forcing it to lie flat. Using the tip of a knife, cut slits in a crosshatch pattern in the cavity anywhere you see bare flesh and make vertical cuts between the ribs, being careful not to cut all the way through.

In a blender, combine 1 cup of the soy sauce, 2 tablespoons of the salt, the garlic, and ginger and blend until smooth. Rub the mixture into every little pocket of the flesh, making sure the skin stays bare and clean. Leave the pig to come to room temperature in an air-conditioned room, 2 to 3 hours.

Prepare a pig roasting box according to the manufacturer's instructions. Lower the pig, skin side down, into the box, being careful to keep the marinade inside the cavity. Roast for 3 hours, adding more charcoal along the way, according to the manufacturer's instructions. In a small bowl, whisk together the oil, distilled white vinegar, and the remaining 2 tablespoons salt.

After 2½ hours of roasting, carefully open the lid and tilt the pig at a 45-degree angle to empty out the liquid that has collected in the cavity. Lay the pig down on its back like before. Using tongs, grasp a clean kitchen towel and use it to blot the cavity of the pig until dry to the touch. Sprinkle the five-spice powder evenly over the cavity. Close the lid and continue to roast for another 30 minutes. The pig should be done at this point, and the internal temperature in the thickest part of the thigh away from bone should register 160° to 165°F.

Open the lid and flip the pig over, skin side up. Using a clean kitchen towel grasped with tongs, blot the skin until dry to the touch. With the pig still secured between the racks, use the tip of a sharp knife to make skin-deep X-shaped slits all over the skin side of the pig. Brush the oil mixture all over the skin and replace the lid. Following the manufacturer's instructions, shake off and discard the ash that has collected under the coals to maximize the heat. Continue to roast the pig, skin side up, for another 30 minutes, lifting one corner of the box just a crack to peek inside after 20 minutes to see how it is doing. As soon as the skin is thoroughly browned, bubbly, and charred, remove the pig from the box and place it on a heatproof surface. Let the pig rest, flesh side down, for 30 minutes.

Meanwhile, prepare the dipping sauce: In a small bowl, combine the remaining 1 cup soy sauce, the pepper flakes, black vinegar, and sugar and stir until the sugar dissolves.

Carve the pig and serve it with the dipping sauce.

NOTE >————————

A suckling pig can be purchased online, but it's likely to be frozen, so be sure to factor the thawing time into your plan. If you have a refrigerator with French doors and the freezer at the bottom, you can clear out your refrigerator in advance to make room for the pig, which should fit just fine. Then let it thaw in the refrigerator for 4 to 5 days. You can also put the pig in an oversize cooler full of ice, changing out the ice along the way until the pig is fully thawed. A frozen suckling pig normally comes already partially split, eviscerated, and cleaned, so it is quite easy to prepare once it is thawed.

ROASTED PORK BELLY ROLL

1 large slab boneless, skin-on pork belly, 10 to 12 pounds

¼ cup coconut, distilled white, or cider vinegar

¼ cup kosher salt

2 tablespoons black peppercorns, coarsely cracked

4 fat lemongrass stalks

1 head garlic, cloves separated and peeled

3 ounces shallots, cubed

2 tablespoons vegetable oil

Of all the celebratory foods of the Philippines, few are held in higher esteem than *lechon*, a roasted suckling pig.

Filipino food expert Tracey Paska tells me there are several regional variations of *lechon*, depending on locally available ingredients and the *lechonero's* (or *lechonera's*) imagination. The two main variations, she explains, are Luzon and Visayan, after the northern and central island groups, respectively, of the Philippine archipelago. While the traditional Luzon *lechon* is seasoned with only salt and pepper, Visayan *lechon* involves stuffing the pig with a variety of herbs and spices, such as garlic, bay leaves, and lots of lemongrass.

But what ties all of these variations together is the preparation of the pig, which is slow roasted on a rotisserie over live coals, and the end goal: copper-colored, glossy, brittle skin. The latter is achieved by occasionally basting the pig with coconut water (a practice I've seen in Bali), soy sauce, or even 7UP. *Lechon* is labor-intensive and costly, and most home cooks, rural or urban, gladly let the pros prepare this feast food, says Paska.

Here we have *lechon liempo*, roasted pork belly roll, a modernized, convenient spin-off of the classic *lechon*. It's still festive, with all the traditional flavors and textures, and it can be prepared at home on a grill. But here's the catch: after testing several methods, I have concluded that for the best result, you should cook the pork belly sous vide before grilling it, and you need to allow three days for the entire process. Roasted pork belly is a decadent, special occasion treat, so you want to do it right.

─── ⟨ **SERVES 8**

Place the pork belly, skin side down, on a work surface. Using the tip of a sharp knife, make slits ½ inch deep in the flesh in a diamond pattern, spacing them about ¾ inch apart. Rub the vinegar, 2 tablespoons of the salt, and the peppercorns into the meat; leave it there for now.

Preheat the sous vide water bath to 160°F, following the manufacturer's instructions.

Meanwhile, trim off the tough outer leaves and the root end from each lemongrass stalk. Beginning from the root end, use a very sharp knife to cut each bulb into thin slices, stopping when the purple rings disappear.

In a small food processor or a mortar, combine the lemongrass, garlic, and shallots and grind to a smooth paste. Rub the paste all over the flesh side of the pork belly and into the slits.

Starting from a long side, roll up the pork belly into a tight roll. Tie the roll with kitchen string, looping it at 1-inch intervals. Place the roll in a large sous vide bag and vacuum seal it, following the manufacturer's instructions. Cook in the prepared water bath for 36 hours.

Prepare a medium-high fire (400° to 450°F) in a charcoal grill using the two-zone method (see page 11).

Remove the pork roll from the bag. Using the tip of a knife, poke several holes into the skin. Blot the outside of the roll with a kitchen towel until dry to the touch. Rub the oil evenly over the skin, then sprinkle the roll evenly with the remaining 2 tablespoons salt.

When the coals are covered with white ash and the grate is hot, put the pork roll on the grate between the hot side and the hold side. The pork is already cooked through at this point (and, if you work quickly, still warm), so all you need to do is to brown and crisp the skin. Cook, with the lid off, rolling the pork between the two zones as needed to prevent burning, until the skin has turned the color of copper, formed tiny bubbles, and crisped all over. This should take 10 to 15 minutes.

Transfer the pork, seam side down, to a wire rack and let rest for 15 minutes. Snip the string, slice about ½ inch thick, and serve.

SATAY OF BABY BACK RIBS
with Peanut Sauce

Even though the lean (and often dry) chicken satay that is a staple at nearly every Thai restaurant in the United States leads people to believe otherwise, the most common type of satay in Thailand by far is made of pork.

A classic pork satay, made on the streets of Thailand, is served with a mild, salty, sweet coconut-based peanut sauce that is redolent of the spices and herbs associated with Thai red or *matsaman* curry. A small, shallow bowl of cool, tangy cucumber salad brings balance to the ensemble, and thick slices of toast, cut into bite-size cubes, are often served alongside.

As far as I know, nobody makes satay with bone-in pork ribs like this. But all of the traditional flavors and components are here. If you miss the bamboo sticks, think of the ribs as pork meat that nature has already threaded onto skewers—here, the rib bones. The big difference is that instead of cooking your satay hot and fast, the way it's typically done, you will need to cook it low and slow.

SERVES 4

To prep the ribs: If the rib racks come with the silvery membrane still attached on the underside, remove it by working a finger underneath the membrane on the larger end of the rack (if necessary, use a chopstick or a butter knife to create a path) and then work your way past two or three ribs toward the opposite end to loosen the membrane. Then, grab the membrane with a paper towel and pull it off decisively and swiftly.

Rub the salt on both sides of the racks. Place the racks on a large sheet pan, cover with plastic wrap, and refrigerate for 2 hours.

Meanwhile, in a dry small frying, combine the coriander, cumin, and fennel seeds over medium-low heat and toast, stirring constantly, until fragrant, 2 to 3 minutes. Transfer the seeds to a spice grinder or a mortar, let cool, and then add the peppercorns and grind to a fine powder. Transfer to a small bowl and stir in the turmeric.

Once the ribs have chilled for 2 hours, moisten both sides of the racks with a little bit of vegetable oil—just enough to form a thin layer of glue for the dry rub—then spread the dry rub evenly on both sides of the racks.

>> CONTINUED

RIBS

2 full racks baby back ribs, about 2 pounds each, rinsed and patted very dry

1½ teaspoons salt

2 tablespoons coriander seeds

1 tablespoon cumin seeds

2 teaspoons fennel seeds

1 tablespoon black peppercorns

2 tablespoons ground turmeric

PEANUT SAUCE

¾ cup unsweetened natural creamy peanut butter (with a layer of oil on top)

¼ cup Thai red or matsaman curry paste

1½ cups unsweetened full-fat coconut milk

½ to ¾ cup granulated sugar

½ cup water

2 tablespoons distilled white or cider vinegar

1½ teaspoons salt

CUCUMBER RELISH

½ cup granulated sugar

½ cup distilled white or cider vinegar

2 tablespoons water

¼ teaspoon salt

½ cup thinly sliced English cucumber

1 ounce shallots, thinly sliced lengthwise

1 fresh Thai long chile, cut crosswise into ¼-inch slices

8 to 10 cilantro leaves

6 slices soft white bread, 1 inch thick, for serving

Prepare a kettle grill for smoking (see page 4) or a pellet grill/smoker (see page 6) according to the manufacturer's instructions. Aim for a temperature between 220° and 230°F. Place the rib racks bone side down in the grill and cook for 2 to 3 hours.

Meanwhile, make the peanut sauce: Pour the oil that has risen to the top of the peanut butter into a 2-quart saucepan (or use ¼ cup peanut or vegetable oil) and heat over medium heat. When the oil is hot, add the curry paste and stir until fragrant, 1 to 2 minutes. Whisk in the peanut butter, coconut milk, ½ cup of the sugar, the water, vinegar, and salt. Bring to a boil and boil gently, whisking often, for 3 minutes. Taste and stir in as much of the remaining sugar as you like. Remove from the heat and let cool until slightly warmer than room temperature.

While the peanut sauce is cooling, prepare the dressing for the cucumber relish: Combine the sugar, vinegar, water, and salt in a small saucepan and bring to gentle boil over medium heat, stirring just until the sugar dissolves. Remove the pan from the heat and let the mixture cool completely.

After 2 hours, begin testing the ribs: Pick up a rack and bend it gently. If the meat between the ribs cracks, you're good to go. Transfer the ribs to a platter but keep the fire going. While the ribs are resting for 10 minutes, toast the bread on both sides on the grill until golden brown and cut it into triangles, halves, or cubes as you wish. Finish the cucumber relish by stirring the cucumber slices, shallot slices, chile slices, and cilantro leaves into the prepared dressing.

Cut the rib racks into individual ribs and serve them with the peanut sauce for dipping, the toast, and the cucumber relish.

GRILLED PORK CHOPS
with Broken Rice and Carrot-Daikon Pickle

This recipe is from my friend Lisa, who has come up with her own way of making her Vietnamese family's favorite, *thit heo nuong xa*. She says it doesn't disappoint, unlike the version served at many restaurants—thin, dry, tough, and buckled in the center. Lisa always knows what she wants. And in this case, she says, closing her eyes and letting out a slow sigh, what she wants is a grilled pork chop—thick and juicy, with a perfectly caramelized crust and succulent and slightly chewy meat around the rib bone. Pork chops, especially thin ones, can be hard to cook well. Some cooks resort to using well-marbled boneless pork shoulder, which is more forgiving, but this doesn't satisfy her second criterion: it has to be a bone-in pork chop, thick and fatty. Her whole family won't eat pork chops prepared any other way now.

Lisa's recipe involves soaking thick-cut pork chops—exactly 2 inches thick with lots of fat still attached—in a pineapple-fish sauce brine. Serve them the traditional way with broken rice and the carrot-daikon pickle, *do chua*. Broken rice is rice of grains that have become fragmented during milling and that cook up a bit sticky yet fluffy. Look for broken rice in Vietnamese and Asian markets.

—————————————————————————————< **SERVES 4**

Make the carrot-daikon pickle: Cut the daikon radish and carrots into thin, 1-inch-long matchsticks. If using regular radishes, thinly slice them crosswise, stack the slices, and cut into thin matchsticks. In a medium bowl, whisk together the warm water, vinegar, granulated sugar, and salt until the sugar and salt dissolve. Put the radish and carrot matchsticks into a clean quart jar and pour the liquid over them, pushing down on the vegetables to submerge them. Cap the jar and refrigerate for 3 days.

The day before serving the meal, brine the pork chops: In a medium bowl, whisk together the pineapple juice, water, fish sauce, soy sauce, and brown sugar until the brown sugar dissolves. Arrange the pork chops in a single layer, not overlapping, in a large baking dish. Pour the brine over the chops, cover with plastic wrap, and refrigerate for 24 hours.

About 1 hour before you grill the pork chops, begin the rice: Put the rice into a fine-mesh sieve and submerge it—sieve and all—in a medium bowl of room-temperature water for 20 minutes.

>> CONTINUED

CARROT-DAIKON PICKLE

4 ounces daikon radish or regular red radishes

4 ounces carrots, peeled

1½ cups lukewarm water

⅓ cup distilled white vinegar

3 tablespoons granulated sugar

1 tablespoon salt

PORK CHOPS

2 cups fresh or canned pineapple juice

1 cup water

⅓ cup fish sauce

¼ cup soy sauce

½ cup packed light brown sugar

4 bone-in pork rib chops, each exactly 2 inches thick

RICE

1¼ cups broken rice

AROMATIC PASTE

2 lemongrass stalks

1 ounce shallots, cubed

2 large garlic cloves

1 tablespoon white or black peppercorns

GREEN ONION OIL

½ cup vegetable oil

1 green onion, trimmed and thinly sliced

FOR SERVING

4 fried eggs (optional)

Tomato slices

Cucumber slices

Lettuce leaves

Meanwhile, make the aromatic paste: Trim off the tough outer leaves and the root end from each lemongrass stalk. Beginning from the root end, use a very sharp knife to cut each bulb into thin slices, stopping when the purple rings disappear. In a small food processor or a mortar, combine the lemongrass, shallots, garlic, and peppercorns and grind to a smooth paste.

Remove the pork chops from the brine and shake the brine off the chops, leaving the surface moist; don't rinse the chops or pat them dry. Discard the brine. Rub the paste all over the pork chops, cover, and leave at room temperature.

Lift the sieve from the bowl of water and, with the rice still in the sieve, rinse the rice under cold running water until the water runs clear; shake off the excess moisture. Transfer the rice to a 2-quart saucepan and, add water to cover by 3 inches. Bring to a boil, uncovered, over high heat, stirring often. Turn down the heat to low, cover, and cook for 3 minutes. Turn off the heat. Open the lid just a crack and pour off all the water, keeping the rice inside the pan. Re-cover the pan tightly and keep the hot rice in the hot pan and let the residual heat continue to steam the rice.

Prepare a medium-high fire (400° to 450°F) in a charcoal grill using the two-zone method (see page 11).

When the coals are covered with white ash and the grate is hot, place the pork chops on the hold side of the grill. Cover and cook with the vents half-opened, flipping once, until the internal temperature in the center of chop registers 120°F, about 10 minutes. Move the chops to the hot side of the grill and cook with the lid off, flipping and moving the chops between the hold and hot sides as a way of controlling the heat and the browning rate of the pork chops. Use tongs to position the chops on their sides so they are browned on the sides as well as the top and bottom. When the pork chops are golden brown and the internal temperature registers 140°F, after 10 to 12 minutes, transfer the pork chops to a large plate. Leave them uncovered while the carryover heat continues to cook them to between 145° and 150°F.

While the chops are resting, quickly make the green onion oil: In a small saucepan, heat the oil on the grill. When the oil is hot, immediately remove the pan from the grill and stir in the green onion.

To serve, fluff the rice and divide it among four plates. Arrange a pork chop on one side of each rice mound, and drizzle the green onion oil over the pork. Put a mound of pickled carrot and daikon on the side. If you want to make the meal extra fancy, put a fried egg on top of the rice, and arrange the tomatoes, cucumber, and lettuce on the side. Serve immediately.

GRILLED PORK SHOULDER
with Spicy Sour-Orange Glaze

Growing citrus trees in Chicagoland where I live is not easy, as they spend several months each year indoors demanding endless pampering: daily exposure to sunlight for a certain number of hours, neither too little nor too much water, nutritional supplements, pruning, pest control, quality time, words of affirmation, and a mani-pedi every month.

But that's what I need to do to have fresh Seville oranges once a year, every year. The way they perfume the kitchen with their fragrant rinds and bestow on me dishes from my childhood that give me Anton Ego–type flashbacks makes all the pain and inconvenience my diva of an orange tree puts me through worth the trouble.

Also known as bitter orange or sour orange, the Seville orange is just as hard to find in the States as it is in Thailand. According to historical records, *som sa*, as it's called in Thai, used to be a common ingredient in Bangkok, but it inexplicably fell into disuse during the last century.

When we sold our great-grandparents' home in Bangkok, one of my aunts transplanted the two Seville orange trees from their backyard to hers to keep them going. She also made sure we all continued to make the dishes that my great-grandmother devised over the years of being blessed with the fruits of those trees. One of them is this recipe, in which grilled pork—tender and smoky—is sauced with a bold, sprightly dressing.

If you can't find Seville oranges, use a combination of navel oranges and limes, as suggested at right. Be sure to pick oranges with hard, thick rinds. They may not be the easiest to juice, but their zest packs more punch.

――――――――――――――――――――――――――――――< SERVES 4 GENEROUSLY

To prep the pork: Prick the pork all over with a fork. In a small bowl, stir together the oil, salt, pepper, and sugar until the sugar dissolves. Rub the oil mixture evenly into the pork. Cover and refrigerate for 2 to 3 hours.

Just before you grill the pork, make the dressing: Stack the citrus zest strips and cut into very thin strips. Transfer to a small bowl, add the orange juice, fish sauce, and chiles, and stir well. Taste and adjust the seasoning as needed, aiming for sour first, then salty, and finally a little bit of sweet. Set aside.

>> CONTINUED

PORK

3 pounds well-marbled boneless pork shoulder steaks, each about ½ inch thick

¼ cup vegetable oil

1 teaspoon salt

1 tablespoon coarsely ground white or black pepper

3 tablespoons packed grated palm sugar or granulated coconut sugar, or 2 tablespoons packed light brown sugar

DRESSING

6 Seville orange zest strips, or 3 strips each lime zest and navel orange zest

¾ cup fresh Seville orange juice, or ½ cup fresh lime juice and ¼ cup fresh navel orange juice

1 tablespoon fish sauce

As many fresh red bird's eye chiles as you can handle, thinly sliced crosswise

Cooked jasmine rice, for serving

Prepare a medium-high fire (400° to 450°F) in a charcoal grill using the two-zone method (see page 11).

When the coals are covered with white ash and the grate is hot, place the pork on the hot side of the grill and cook with the lid off, controlling the heat by moving the pork back and forth from the hot side to the hold side, until charred on the outside and the internal temperature registers 145°F. Transfer to a cutting board and let rest for 5 to 7 minutes.

Cut the pork against the grain into ½-inch-thick slices. Arrange the slices in a single layer on a platter. Pour the dressing over the pork. Serve with the rice.

BARBECUED PORK

This type of barbecued pork is an everyday food in Southeast Asia. It's similar to Cantonese-style barbecued pork, or *char siu*, which is found in Chinatowns throughout North America, and in most cases, the differences are negligible. But Southeast Asian–style barbecued pork is typically less sweet, less glossy, and less about the hoisin sauce and more about red fermented bean curd and salted fermented soybeans.

Red fermented bean curd is a pungent and salty condiment and seasoning made by fermenting bean curd (tofu) cubes in seasoned brine with the addition of red yeast rice, which gives it its signature color. It comes packed in brine in a glass jar and is available at most Asian stores and online. The bean curd is very soft and can be mashed into a smooth paste easily with the back of a spoon.

I like to make my *mu daeng*, as this pork is known in Thailand, in a barrel cooker (see page 6), where the pork hangs over smoldering coals inside a steel drum and comes out incredibly juicy and smoky without me having to babysit it. And when the pork is cooked low and slow this way, the meat naturally turns dark reddish brown, eliminating the need for the red food coloring that most vendors use.

2 tablespoons mashed red fermented tofu, plus 2 tablespoons liquid from the jar

2 tablespoons mashed salted fermented soybeans

2 tablespoons oyster sauce

2 tablespoons soy sauce

2 tablespoons Shaoxing rice wine (see Note, page 126)

3 tablespoons granulated sugar

2 thumb-size pieces fresh ginger, peeled and juiced to yield 2 tablespoons juice

5 large garlic cloves, pressed or finely minced to a paste

3 pounds well-marbled boneless pork shoulder

¼ cup honey

―――――――――――――――――――――――――――――――――――――< **SERVES 4**

In a large bowl, combine the fermented bean curd and its liquid, fermented soybeans, oyster sauce, soy sauce, wine, sugar, ginger juice, and garlic paste; stir until the sugar dissolves and all the ingredients are well blended. Cut the pork shoulder into thick strips. It doesn't matter much how long the strips are, but they need to be 3 to 3½ inches thick. Add the pork to the bowl and mix well. Cover and refrigerate overnight.

Prepare a barrel cooker according to the manufacturer's instructions. If using a kettle grill, fill a chimney with coals. Spread half of the unlit coals on one side of the grill, leaving the other half in the chimney. Place a quarter-size disposable foil pan, half-filled with water, on the side without coals. Light the coals left in the chimney. When the coals are covered with white ash, pour them over the unlit coals in the grill.

Shake the marinade off the pork strips, letting the liquid drip back into the bowl. Reserve ¾ cup of the marinade and discard the rest. If using a barrel cooker, hang the pork over the coals, close the lid, and let it cook undisturbed until the internal temperature registers 135°F, 1½ to 2 hours. If using a kettle grill, place the pork on the hold side of the grill over the water pan and cook

>> CONTINUED

NOTE >————————————

Made by fermenting glutinous rice, amber-colored Shaoxing wine, which originated in eastern China, has a complex aroma and flavor and is used for both cooking and drinking. This is a common ingredient that can be easily purchased from most Asian stores and online.

with the lid on until the internal temperature registers 135°F, 1½ to 2 hours. Along the way, adjust the vents as needed to maintain the temperature at 250° to 275°F.

Meanwhile, make the glaze: In a small bowl, stir together the reserved marinade and the honey.

When the pork is ready, remove it from the cooker or the grill, keeping the fire going. Quickly brush the glaze all over the pork and return the pork to the cooker or to the hold side of the grill and continue to cook until the internal temperature registers 145°F and the glaze has set into a lightly charred crust on the surface of the pork, 10 to 15 minutes. Transfer to a cutting board and let rest for 15 minutes.

Slice the pork against the grain and serve.

SPICY GRILLED PORK SALAD

2 pounds well-marbled
boneless pork shoulder

1 tablespoon packed
grated palm sugar or
granulated coconut sugar,
or 2 teaspoons packed
light brown sugar

1 teaspoon salt

2 tablespoons Thai glutinous
rice (see headnote, page 56)

½ cup chicken stock

2 tablespoons fish sauce

¼ cup very thinly sliced
shallots

¼ cup fresh lime juice

Red pepper flakes, for
seasoning

¼ cup roughly chopped fresh
cilantro leaves and stems

½ cup loosely packed fresh
mint leaves

3 to 4 dried red bird's eye
chiles, for garnish

2 or 3 wedges green
cabbage, for serving

Cooked sticky rice
(see page 56) or jasmine rice,
for serving

Lightly marinated pork shoulder, grilled over hot coals just until
smoky and charred on the outside and barely pink on the inside, is a
good eat. But sliced up and doused with dressing—a beautiful interplay
of fragrant herbs, funky fish sauce, vibrant lime juice, smoky dried
chiles, and nutty ground toasted rice—it becomes the glorious *nam tok
mu*, a beloved classic from northeastern Thailand.

This dish is cooked twice quickly—but twice nonetheless. So it's
important to use the right cut of pork: nothing too lean, like pork loin
or tenderloin, or too fatty or too tough to eat (unless slow cooked), like
pork belly. Well-marbled boneless pork shoulder is your Goldilocks. If
you ask me, nothing else will do.

This grilled pork salad is served warm—neither piping hot nor at
room temperature—traditionally with sticky rice.

SERVES 4

Cut the pork into large slices ½ inch thick. Prick each slice a few times with
a fork. In a medium bowl, stir together the sugar and salt. Add the pork and
rub the sugar mixture evenly into the strips. Cover and refrigerate for 3 to
4 hours.

Meanwhile, in a dry small frying pan, toast the rice over medium-low heat,
stirring almost constantly, until the grains are golden brown and have a
nutty aroma, about 15 minutes. Immediately transfer the rice to a small
heatproof bowl and let cool completely (do not leave it in the pan, as it will
continue to toast). In a small food processor or a mortar, grind the rice to
a coarse powder. Measure out 2 tablespoons for serving; discard the rest or
keep it for a future use.

Light a full chimney of charcoal. When the coals are ready, spread them out
on the bottom of a kettle grill or hibachi for cooking over a high fire.

When the coals are covered with white ash and the grate is hot, place the
pork on the grate and cook (with the lid off if using a kettle grill), flipping
often, until lightly but thoroughly charred on the outside yet still rare
on the inside, 5 to 6 minutes. Transfer to a plate, cover, and let rest for
15 minutes.

Cut the pork against the grain into bite-size slices about ¼ inch thick.
Transfer the slices along with any accumulated juices to a 2-quart saucepan
(one that is wide and shallow works better than one that is narrow and

>> CONTINUED

deep). Add the stock, set it over medium-high heat, and heat, stirring often. When the liquid forms tiny bubbles around the edge of the pan, add the fish sauce and stir briskly to make sure every piece of pork is cooked—though ever so lightly. Immediately remove the pan from the heat and, while everything is still warm, stir in the shallots and lime juice. Taste and adjust the seasoning with more fish sauce and lime juice. Keep in mind that this is not a delicately seasoned salad—northeastern Thai dishes typically pack a punch! You want it predominantly sour, then salty, with a faint sweetness from the natural pork juice and what's left of the sugar in the marinade. Also, don't forget that you're eating this with bland rice, so season accordingly.

Once it tastes good to you, decide how spicy hot you want it and stir in as much pepper flakes as you like. Now, quickly stir in the cilantro and 1 tablespoon of the toasted rice and stir vigorously to wilt the herbs slightly and disperse the rice evenly.

Arrange the salad on a platter. Sprinkle the remaining 1 tablespoon toasted rice on top, followed by the mint leaves. Garnish with the dried chiles, which you can crumble into the salad for extra heat. Serve immediately with the cabbage and enjoy with warm rice.

PORK BELLY BURNT ENDS

My friend Jem grew up in one of the many families of Hokkien Chinese who came from the Fujian Province in southeastern China and were settled and assimilated into Thailand, mostly on the southern Thai island of Phuket. He recently taught me how to make a classic Hokkien Thai favorite, *mu hong*, a comfort dish of braised pork belly, tender, sweet and salty, and fragrant of warm spices.

It was interesting to me how many times Jem used the word "smoke" while showing me how he made this heirloom family recipe. As good as his version was, said Jem apologetically, it was not nearly as memorable as his late grandmother's, who always made hers on a wood-charcoal stove—the kind most modern cooks in urban areas no longer use. "It's the smoke," Jem said. "The smoke makes everything good—it sticks so well to fatty meat like this, and it makes everything better."

That day, as I stood next to Jem stirring a pot of pork belly on an electric cooktop in my Bangkok condo, I mentally concocted a plan to try and make this dish in the smoker in the backyard of my home in Chicagoland. I took a cue from pit masters who substitute pork belly when making the classic brisket burnt ends of Kansas City. The pork belly yields tender, succulent little bites in much the same way as the point end of a brisket because of the high fat content. I wanted to know what would happen if I combined that approach with the spices and traditional seasoning ingredients in Hokkien Thai braised dishes. After many experiments, I've come up with this recipe, which creates the classic *mu hong* of Phuket—except it's extra smoky and, according to Jem, extra delicious. In addition to a smoker, you will need two 9 by 13-inch disposable aluminum pans about 2 inches deep.

SERVES 8

To prep the pork: Rub the pork with the oil. In a large bowl, stir together the brown sugar, five-spice powder, salt, and pepper. Add the pork to the bowl and rub the sugar mixture on all sides; cover and refrigerate for 1 hour.

Meanwhile, prepare a pellet grill/smoker by filling a heatproof bowl with water and placing the bowl to one side of the grate (alternatively, prepare a vertical water smoker according to the manufacturer's instructions. Aim for a temperature of 250°F.

>> CONTINUED

PORK

5 pounds skinless pork belly, cut into 2-inch cubes

3 tablespoons vegetable oil

¼ cup packed light brown sugar

2 tablespoons Chinese five-spice powder

2 teaspoons salt

2 teaspoons ground white or black pepper

SAUCE

6 large garlic cloves

3 cilantro roots, finely chopped, or 3 tablespoons finely chopped fresh cilantro stems stripped of leaves

2 teaspoons white or black peppercorns

3 tablespoons vegetable oil

¾ cup packed grated palm sugar or granulated coconut sugar, or ½ cup packed light brown sugar

2 tablespoons coconut, distilled white, or cider vinegar

2 cups chicken stock

1 to 2 tablespoons fish sauce

2 tablespoons Shaoxing rice wine (see Note, page 126)

2 cinnamon sticks

4 star anise pods

3 or 4 grinds white or black pepper, for serving

Cooked long-grain rice, for serving

Arrange the pork, fat side down, on the smoker grate, spacing the cubes about ½ inch apart. Smoke, replenishing the water bowl as needed, until the belly forms a nice "bark" on the outside and registers an internal temperature of 170°F, 2½ to 3 hours. At this point, the belly is not going to be meltingly tender, but it will be cooked once more and become more tender. (Besides, I, like most Thai people, prefer the pork belly to have a bit of "bite" to it. If you want your pork belly fall-apart tender, go for 180° to 190°F.)

While the pork cooks, make the sauce: In a mortar, pound the garlic, cilantro roots, and peppercorns to a smooth paste. In a 12-inch skillet, heat the oil over medium heat. When the oil is hot (but not smoking), add the paste and fry, stirring constantly, until fragrant, about 1 minute. Stir in the palm sugar, vinegar, and stock, and turn up the heat to high. Bring to a boil, and boil uncovered, stirring often, until the liquid reduces to about 1½ cups, about 10 minutes. At this point, the sauce will need some salinity apart from the little bit that you get from the stock, so add the fish sauce to taste, starting with a couple of teaspoons. Aim for a flavor that is equally salty and sweet, with a bit of sour trailing behind. Remove from the heat, stir in the wine, cinnamon sticks, and star anise, and set aside.

Remove the pork from the smoker and divide it between the two disposable pans, spreading the cubes in a single layer. Divide the sauce (including the cinnamon sticks and star anise) evenly between the pans and toss until the pork cubes are evenly coated.

Crank the smoker up to 300°F. Cover the pans tightly with aluminum foil and put them into the smoker. Cook until the internal temperature registers 180°F if you like the pork a bit chewy (about an hour) or 200° to 210°F if you prefer it fall-apart tender (about 1½ hours).

Remove the foil, close the smoker lid, and smoke for another 15 to 20 minutes to reduce the sauce to a tight glaze. Remove from the smoker and leave to rest 15 minutes.

Remove and discard the cinnamon and star anise and transfer the pork to a platter. Dust the pork with the pepper and serve with the rice.

GRILLED PORK SKEWERS

with Spicy Dipping Vinegar

PORK

¼ cup fresh calamansi juice (see Note, page 79) or lemon juice

½ cup banana or tomato ketchup

¼ cup packed light brown sugar

¾ cup lemon-lime soda (such as 7UP), chilled

¼ cup soy sauce

½ teaspoon salt

4 large garlic cloves, minced

1 teaspoon ground black pepper

2 pounds well-marbled boneless pork shoulder, thinly sliced against the grain into bite-size pieces

DIPPING VINEGAR

½ cup distilled white vinegar

2 tablespoons soy sauce

1 ounce shallots, coarsely chopped

1 large garlic clove, finely chopped

3 or 4 fresh red bird's eye chiles, sliced

Garlic rice (see page 79) or plain cooked long-grain rice, for serving

I first had these Filipino-style grilled pork skewers many years ago when I was attending a conference at the University of Philippines Diliman in Quezon City. It was a weeklong conference with breakfast, lunch, and dinner catered by the host group. At exactly fourteen meals out of twenty-one—I counted—these grilled pork skewers, which everyone there called "pork barbecue," showed up in one of the chafing dishes. It was obvious that either someone in charge of the menu planning really, really liked the dish, or that it was so well loved over there that repeating that often was more a way to please the diners than to bore them. Both were the case, according to one of the servers, who revealed that the ingredients include banana ketchup and lemon-lime soda. I've been making this dish ever since.

The practice of using the combination of lemon-lime soda, ketchup, soy sauce, and the juice of calamansi as a marinade and basting sauce for pork barbecue became popular in the 1970s among street-food vendors in the Philippines. The citrus-forward mixture was believed to hide the stench of meat that was exposed to the elements, and the carbonation helped tenderize cheap, tough cuts, explains food historian Ige Ramos. As for banana ketchup, its invention is credited to Filipino food technologist Maria Y. Orosa, who was prompted by a shortage of tomato ketchup during World War II. According to Ramos, most Filipinos prefer the sweet banana ketchup over tangy tomato ketchup, and it's so popular among the masses that even homegrown fast-food joints give out sachets of banana ketchup with their burgers.

Banana ketchup, which is made from banana puree, sugar, and spices, can be found at most well-stocked Asian grocery stores or online (the most popular brand is Jufran). If you can't find it, use tomato ketchup.

SERVES 4

Soak eight 12-inch bamboo skewers in water to cover for 1 to 2 hours.

To prep the pork: In a large bowl, stir together the calamansi juice, ketchup, sugar, soda, soy sauce, salt, garlic, and pepper. Add the pork and mix well. Cover and refrigerate for at least 8 hours or up to overnight.

Before grilling the pork, make the vinegar: In a small bowl, stir together the vinegar, soy sauce, shallots, garlic, and chiles. Set aside to mellow until serving time.

Prepare a medium-high fire (400° to 450°F) in a charcoal grill using the two-zone method (see page 11).

Thread the pork onto the soaked skewers (see page 93). When the coals are covered with white ash and the grate is hot, set the pork on the hot side of the grill and cook with the lid off, turning often, until the meat is well charred on the outside, 6 to 7 minutes. Move the skewers closer to the hold side of the grill, cover, and cook with the vents slightly opened, turning often, until the meat is just cooked through, 5 to 7 minutes longer.

Transfer the skewers to a platter and serve with the rice and dipping vinegar.

PORK AND CRABMEAT CRÉPINETTES

with Pineapple-Chile Dipping Sauce

CRÉPINETTES

5 large garlic cloves

2 cilantro roots, chopped, or 2 tablespoons finely chopped cilantro stems stripped of leaves

2 teaspoons white or black peppercorns

2 pounds cold ground pork

1 pound claw crabmeat (see Note), picked over for shell fragments

2 tablespoons soy sauce

1 tablespoon oyster sauce

Salt

12 ounces caul fat (see photo, opposite), soaked in lukewarm water to cover for 15 minutes (optional)

SAUCE

6 fresh red bird's eye chiles, or 2 red jalapeño or serrano peppers, cut into small pieces

4 large garlic cloves

1 small pineapple, about 1¼ pounds

½ cup granulated sugar

¼ cup distilled white or cider vinegar

1½ teaspoons salt

1 tablespoon cornstarch mixed with 2 tablespoons water

Red pepper flakes, for garnish

Cooked jasmine rice, for serving

This recipe is the result of my experimenting on *pu ja*, a classic Chinese Thai dish of pork and crabmeat sausage packed into empty crab shells, steamed, and deep-fried. Instead of following the lead of every seaside restaurant in Thailand and using crab shells as the sausage vessels, I wrap the sausage meat in lacy caul fat, *crépine* in French, to create small parcels. The idea was inspired by *hati babi bungkus*, pork meatballs wrapped in caul fat and grilled, a classic dish of the Peranakan people of Malaysia and Singapore. Their hybrid cuisine, known as Nonya (Nyonya) or Peranakan, is a blending of Chinese and the indigenous Malay cooking traditions. I serve my version of *pu ja* with a sweet chile sauce made with pineapple, a substitute for the Chinese plums (*Prunus mume*), aka Japanese apricots, used in the traditional plum sauce accompaniment.

These sausage parcels are to be served with rice, but if you form the sausage mixture into balls and flatten them into burger-size patties, you can serve them on sticky rice "buns" (page 141) as burgers.

Caul fat is the thin, lacy membrane surrounding the pig's internal organs. It is used as a casing for sausages or pâtés because it holds the ground meat together in a nice, compact package and it brings moisture to the dish as the fat renders during cooking. It is a specialty ingredient, so you may have to source it online, as it can be difficult to find locally. If you can't locate it, skip it and make sure the sausage patties are compact and tight and not loosey-goosey.

———————————————————————— **SERVES 4**

To prep the crépinettes: In a small food processor or a mortar, combine the garlic, cilantro roots, and peppercorns and grind to a smooth paste. Transfer to a large bowl, add the pork, crabmeat, soy sauce, and oyster sauce, and knead together until sticky. Cook a couple of teaspoons of the mixture in a small frying pan over medium heat or in a microwave, then taste and adjust the seasoning of the mixture with salt if needed. Cover and refrigerate for at least 4 hours or up to overnight.

To make the sauce: In a small food processor, blend the chiles and garlic until the bits are the size of a match head. Transfer to a 1-quart saucepan. Peel and core the pineapple and cut the flesh into 1-inch cubes. Measure out only 2 cups and blend in the food processor into a smooth purée. Transfer to the saucepan and add the sugar, vinegar, and salt. Bring to a boil over medium heat, whisking often, then adjust the heat to a simmer and cook for

5 minutes to blend the flavors. Add the cornstarch slurry and cook, whisking constantly, for 1 minute. Remove from the heat, cover, and let cool.

Remove the caul fat from the water, shake off the excess moisture, and lay it out flat on a large cutting board or a cut-resistant countertop. Divide the sausage meat into sixteen equal portions and shape each portion into a ½-inch-thick patty with smooth edges. Put a patty on the caul fat, positioning it near one corner of the sheet. Using the tip of a sharp paring knife, cut the caul fat around the patty into a square. The square should be big enough to wrap the patty completely without overlapping too much in the middle. Wrap the caul fat around the patty and place the patty, seam side down, on a sheet pan. Repeat with the remaining patties. If you have more caul fat than you need, fold it up and freeze it for another use.

Prepare a medium-high fire (400° to 450°F) in a charcoal grill using the two-zone method (see page 11). When the coals are covered with white ash and the grate is hot, place the crépinettes on the hot side of the grill and cook uncovered, flipping every 30 seconds, just until they develop some color on both sides, about 3 minutes. Move them to the hold side and cook with lid on and the vents half-opened, flipping them a couple of times, until the internal temperature registers 145°F, about 7 minutes. Transfer to a platter and let rest for 5 minutes.

Meanwhile, check on the sauce, which may have thickened on cooling. It should have the consistency of ketchup, so if it's too thick, stir in some water. Garnish the crépinettes with the chiles and cilantro and serve with the rice and dipping sauce.

NOTE >———————

If money is no object, use lump crabmeat. But it is not really necessary to use premium crabmeat in this dish.

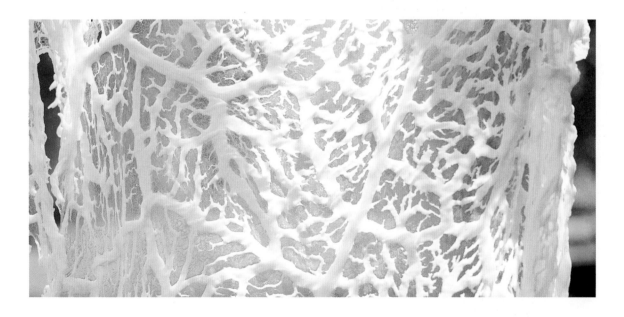

GRILLED PORK–STICKY RICE BURGERS

This recipe was inspired by the sticky rice burgers at 7-Eleven Thailand. It combines northeastern Thai–style meat salad (*lap* or, as popularly spelled, *larb*) and sticky rice in a Western invention that's well loved the world over: the hamburger.

The sticky rice "buns" are held together with nothing more than the natural amylopectin in the rice grains, the starch that makes it glutinous or sticky. Thus, it's important that you use the correct type of rice (see headnote, page 56) and that you cook it the right way. Also, once the rice is fully cooked, be careful not to introduce too much moisture to it; if the cooked grains take on moisture, they will lose the "glue" that holds them together. This is the reason I think you should do what 7-Eleven does, which is to season your pork patties so amply that your burgers don't need even a thin smear of sauce—or, in fact, anything else at all. Keeping the burgers small and the patties flat, diner-style, also makes it easier both to assemble and to eat them. You'll need a burger press or a brick wrapped in foil to flatten them and eight 4-inch egg rings.

1½ pounds cold ground pork

1 ounce shallots, minced

2 tablespoons fish sauce

¼ cup fresh lime juice

1 teaspoon red pepper flakes

2 tablespoons finely chopped fresh cilantro leaves and stems

1 tablespoon finely chopped fresh mint leaves

Cooked sticky rice (see page 56), kept warm

———————————————————————————⟨ **SERVES 4**

In a medium bowl, combine the pork, shallots, fish sauce, lime juice, and pepper flakes and knead until sticky. Cook a couple teaspoons of the mixture in a small frying pan over medium heat or in a microwave, then taste and adjust the seasoning of the mixture with more lime juice or fish sauce if needed. The meat should be equally salty and sour and seasoned heavily enough for the bland rice. Cover and refrigerate for at least 4 hours or up to overnight.

Prepare a medium-high fire (400° to 450°F) in a charcoal grill using the two-zone method (see page 11).

Knead the cilantro and mint into the meat mixture, making sure they are evenly distributed. Form the meat into eight patties, each slightly more than 4 inches in diameter. Have ready a burger press or an aluminum foil–covered brick.

When the coals are covered with white ash and the grate is hot, place the patties on the hot side of the grill. Cook uncovered, pressing down on the patties with the press or brick to keep them flat, until browned on both sides and cooked through, about 7 minutes. Transfer to a plate and keep warm.

>> CONTINUED

Have ready eight 4-inch egg rings. Working quickly and with very lightly moistened hands, pack half of the sticky rice into the eight egg rings, pressing down just until you have a compact ring of rice with the grains still visible and distinct. Repeat to make eight more "buns." Quickly assemble the burgers by placing one patty between two buns. Enjoy immediately.

Any leftovers can be wrapped in plastic wrap and refrigerated for up to 3 days. The only way you can reheat them is in a microwave (which is what 7-Eleven stores in Thailand do). The burgers can also be frozen, but you have to thaw them completely in the fridge before microwaving them.

GRILLED PORK SAUSAGE JERKY

In Malaysia and Singapore, where this dish is known as *bak kwa*, it's enjoyed as an everyday food, a celebration food, and even as a souvenir. It's also well loved in Chinese communities throughout Southeast Asia. The sweet and lightly spiced jerky is not dehydrated like most jerky. It's cooked in sheet form all the way through and then finished on the grill, where it becomes caramelized and smoky.

Chinese rose wine is a sweetened, cereal grain–based wine infused with rose essence, sold in most Asian markets and online. A little bit of it goes a long way in providing the subtle yet intoxicating fragrance to food.

I like to eat *bak kwa* with plain rice or rice porridge, but you can eat it as a stand-alone snack (if this is your plan, reduce the amount of soy sauce and fish sauce somewhat so it doesn't taste too salty). That said, a friend of mine likes to tear *mu phaen* (as it's known in Thailand) into pieces and add it to fried rice, while another friend likes to shred it and add it to spicy vegetable salad. On a trip to Singapore, I had a pizza topped with *bak kwa*. So feel free to get creative with how you enjoy this otherwise very traditional dish. Modern cooks in Southeast Asia certainly do.

2 pounds well-marbled boneless pork shoulder, cut into tiny cubes and chilled

¼ cup granulated sugar

½ cup packed light brown sugar

2 teaspoons ground white or black pepper

1 teaspoon Chinese five-spice powder

2 tablespoons oyster sauce

2 tablespoons soy sauce

2 tablespoons fish sauce

1 tablespoon Chinese rose wine (mei kuei lu chiew), or 2 tablespoons Shaoxing rice wine (see Note, page 126)

½ cup honey

———————————————————⊰ **MAKES A GENEROUS 1 POUND**

In a food processor, combine the pork, both sugars, pepper, five-spice powder, oyster sauce, soy sauce, fish sauce, and wine and process until the mixture is very sticky, with a texture similar to Italian bulk sausage. (You may need to do this in batches, depending on the capacity of your food processor bowl.) Scrape the mixture into a medium bowl. Cover and refrigerate for 2 hours.

Position a rack in the middle of the oven and preheat the oven to 325°F.

Cut two 13 by 18-inch sheets of parchment paper. Place one sheet on a countertop. Form the sausage meat into a large ball and set it on the center of the paper. Use your hands to shape the sausage ball into a rectangular mound. Place the second sheet of parchment on top of the mound and, using a rolling pin, roll the sausage mound into a rectangle about ⅛ inch thick. The rectangle doesn't need to have straight sides, specific dimensions, or be perfectly symmetrical. Peel off the top sheet of parchment. Use a moistened hand or spatula to smooth the edges of the meat sheet.

Using the bottom parchment sheet, lift up the pork sausage sheet and place it, still on the paper, on a large sheet pan. Brush the top of the sausage sheet

>> CONTINUED

with half of the honey. Bake for 10 minutes. Flip the sausage sheet over onto the same sheet pan so the parchment is now on top. Peel off the parchment. Wipe off any excess moisture and fat from the surface of the sausage sheet and brush it with the remaining honey. Return the pan to the oven and bake for another 10 minutes. At this point, the sausage sheet should be cooked through. Transfer the pan to a rack and let the sausage sheet cool completely.

When the sheet is cool, leave it on the sheet pan. Using the tip of a sharp knife or a pizza cutter, trim off any edges that turned too dark during baking, then cut the sheet into 3-inch squares. Set a large rack on a second large sheet pan. Using a thin metal spatula, carefully lift the squares, one at a time, off the pan and place them on the rack. Refrigerate until dry to the touch, about 8 hours or up to overnight.

Prepare a medium-high fire (400° to 450°F) in a charcoal grill using the two-zone method (see page 11).

When the coals are covered with white ash and the grate is hot, oil the grate. Place the squares in the middle of the grill where the hot side meets the hold side. Grill the squares with the lid off, flipping them often with tongs and being extremely watchful as they burn easily. When the squares are thoroughly browned and blistered on both sides and charred around the edges, after 3 to 4 minutes per side, transfer them to a wire rack. Leave to cool completely.

Store the jerky in an airtight container in the refrigerator for up to 1 week.

HOW TO STUFF SAUSAGE

To stuff sausage, start with natural casings. These can be found at most butcher shops, most supermarkets specializing in European — especially eastern European — ingredients, and many mainstream grocery stores. Hog casings are the most traditional choice and the most widely available. Sheep casings, though they aren't normally used in Southeast Asia, work as well, but they are not as easy to find. I don't recommend any casing other than these two.

To prepare salted natural casings, soak them for 1 hour in cold water to cover, changing the water every 15 minutes. Drain well, then, working with one length of casing at a time, gently pull one end of the casing over the spout of the kitchen sink faucet. Turn the water on low and let it flow gently through the casing for about 1 minute to rinse the inside well. Repeat with the remaining casings. (Any unused casings can be packed in salt again and kept refrigerated. When well covered in salt, natural hog casings will stay fresh for up to 1 year in the refrigerator.)

For home use, nothing beats a vertical, single-gear sausage stuffer, which is equipped with a piston with a release valve that lets the air escape, making an otherwise annoying task fun. This type of stuffer is compatible with multiple sizes of stuffing tubes. For the sausage recipes in this book, you will be using a 1-inch tube, which produces sausages about the size of fresh Italian ones. A distant second-best choice, in my experience, is the sausage stuffer attachment that comes with some makes and models of stand mixers. To stuff sausage with a vertical sausage stuffer or a stand mixer attachment, follow the manufacturer's instructions.

If you don't have a good sausage stuffer, you can try the homespun method that many home cooks in Southeast Asia use. It involves pushing the sausage meat into the casing through a funnel with the handle of a wooden spoon — or any object that fits inside the funnel's narrow end. I personally don't like this method, but it works fine. It is labor-intensive and time-consuming, however, so it isn't the best method when you are making a large batch — and, let's face it, sausage is not something you usually make in small batches.

A better compromise is to use a piping bag. All you have to do is fit the plastic piping bag with a ½-inch round tip and then fill the bag half full with the sausage meat. Cut the casings into 2-foot lengths and knot one end of each length. Pull the open end of a length of casing over the tip of the piping bag. Use one hand to squeeze the bag and the other hand to grip firmly around the part of the bag where the tip is covered with the casing end. Pipe slowly and refill the bag along the way. Prick the sausages with a pin wherever an air pocket forms.

How tightly you should stuff sausage casings depends on the type of sausage and how it's linked. Since you will be twisting or tying the links by hand for the recipes in this book, which can put uneven stress on the casing, stuff to about ¹⁄₁₀ inch less than the maximum expansion of the casing. By understuffing, there is less chance of the sausage breaking when you twist or tie the links.

GRILLED NORTHEASTERN THAI SOURED SAUSAGE

6 cilantro roots, chopped, or 6 tablespoons finely chopped fresh cilantro stems stripped of leaves

25 large garlic cloves

2 tablespoons black peppercorns

2 tablespoons white peppercorns

4½ pounds coarsely ground pork

8 ounces fatback, finely diced (see Note, page 151)

1 level teaspoon pink curing salt #1 (see Note, page 170)

3 tablespoons salt

½ cup room-temperature water

2 cups cooked sticky rice (see page 56) or long-grain rice, at room temperature

4 ounces hog casings, soaked in lukewarm water (90°F) to cover for 1 hour

FOR SERVING

Green lettuce leaves

Thin fresh ginger slices

Fresh bird's eye chiles

Unsalted roasted peanuts

Shallots, quartered

I can never matter-of-factly talk about this sausage because it is not just any sausage to me—and it has never been. Yes, it is one of the favorites among fans of regional Thai foods across the world, all of whom pride themselves on knowing obscure Thai dishes. Yes, in my opinion, this fermented sausage is indeed one of the most delicious things that has come out of Thailand's northeastern region of Isan. And yes, it is not the easiest thing to make well, even though the procedure is quite simple. But it is a sausage nonetheless, and—goodness gracious—do we *need* to romanticize a sausage?

I feel like I'm introducing a dear friend to you. But if we need to leave the realm of anthropomorphism and get back to real life and real people, I would also add that the inclusion of this recipe here is a fulfillment of the yearning of someone who means a great deal to me.

Nearly a decade ago, on the day my cousins and I were clearing out our great-grandparents' World War II–era teakwood home in Bangkok to prepare it for the exterminators, we didn't expect to discover anything in the attic other than perhaps a colony of well-fed termites. Instead, we found an old note, which became the genesis of the recipe you are now reading.

A handwritten note, addressed to our late grandmother, was wedged between the pages of an old Thai entertainment magazine, where the Bangkok release of a new Hollywood movie, *Superman* starring Christopher Reeve, was announced.

Written in the northeastern dialect and with penmanship bad enough to send the most self-assured of epigraphers into a state of despair, the note was a nightmare to decipher. However, once a quick scan revealed a recipe was involved, I immediately put on my philologist hat and got to work.

The note turned out to be from an acquaintance of our grandparents, who said he was too old and tired to continue his sausage business and thought he'd pass on his recipe to our grandmother, as she'd been begging him for it for years. Right away, we realized this was the man whom Grandma often praised as the most skillful maker of what northeastern Thais call *sai krok priao* (sour sausage), referred to by those outside the region as *sai krok isan* (Isan sausage). It was the

>> CONTINUED

recipe Grandma had misplaced upon receipt, a loss she'd mourned throughout the latter part of her life. Little did she know that, since 1978, her lost treasure was inside a magazine, lying intimately against the Man of Steel's gloriously red undies.

Although not from the northeast, Grandma had eaten the best the region had to offer. Spending her formative years in a northeastern province where her father served as governor, she understood northeastern Thai culture and cuisine very well. My grandmother often spoke in glowing terms about the taste and texture of northeastern delicacies such as *mam*, a fermented sausage made with chopped beef and beef innards and stuffed into a cow's bladder. She also spoke of what properly made *sai krok isan* was like, and how superior it was to many poorly made ones found all over Bangkok—the ones my generation have come to regard as typical. And if she considered a sausage maker worthy of being elevated above many in Isan, we knew we'd better pay attention.

But, as if a joke, the hard work of deciphering that old note produced nothing but a generic recipe for this quintessential northeastern fermented sausage. It didn't call for out-of-the-ordinary ingredients or require an obscure technique. You simply mix together meat, fat, garlic, cooked rice, and salt; stuff the paste into casings; ferment; and grill. I asked the world what it usually yawned at, and it sleepily pointed to a recipe like that one.

The recipe is not entirely without a redeeming factor, however. The key to achieving great quality *sai krok isan*—quite possibly the very reason instructions from this person meant so much to Grandma— is found in the concluding sentence, which loosely translated reads, "Don't put in more rice than meat; the rice must not be seen!!!!!" One could say this is merely one cook's opinion, the dogmatic tone and excessive use of exclamation points notwithstanding, and that would be correct. But after giving this earnest remark some thought, I've come to see the wisdom of it.

Cooked rice is used in this dish merely as the agent for fermentation; it's supposed to disintegrate and fade away; its presence isn't meant to compete with that of the main ingredient, pork. Is this some sort of a prophetic utterance about the present-day sausage vendors' unscrupulous use of cheap fillers? If you've visited Thailand in recent years, you may have even come across a somewhat new variation of *sai krok isan* containing copious amounts of glass (bean thread) noodles. While this variation has certainly become popular, one can't help but wonder whether it represents a clever twist on a classic dish or just another way in which vendors cope with the rising cost of ingredients.

Most traditional Thai cured meat recipes don't call for any additives, and this one is no different. Meats have been cured at home this way for ages—in hot and humid climates of Southeast Asia no less. Regardless, the use of sodium nitrite to keep products safe from harmful bacteria is common among manufacturers for obvious reasons.

This is my best shot at *sai krok isan*. It's simple and traditional, with no added yeasts or enzymes to manipulate the fermentation. The inclusion of pink salt is here for your safety, following the guidelines of the National Center for Home Food Preservation. The sausages hang at room temperature for up to a week, so omit it at your own risk. But keep in mind that if you do, the sausages will look unappetizingly grayish inside, though they will taste the same.

——————————————< **MAKES ABOUT 5 POUNDS; SERVES 6 TO 8**

In a food processor, combine the cilantro roots, garlic, and both the peppercorns and process to a smooth paste. Transfer to a very clean, large bowl along with the pork and fatback. With gloved or immaculately clean hands, mix together everything well. Dissolve the curing salt and the salt in the water, add to the mixture, and mix well. Add the rice and mix until well blended and sticky.

Stuff the sausage meat into the casings (see page 145). You can tie or twist them into either 4-inch links or 1-inch balls. Hang them at room temperature to ferment and dry out until the sausage is sour enough for you. In a cold climate, it could take up to a week. In a warmer climate, 3 or 4 days should be sufficient time. If this is your first time making this sausage, you may want to tie the sausage into a rope of 1-inch balls. That way, you can cook one up along the way to taste for sourness without wasting too much sausage. Properly soured *sai krok isan* should have the savory tang generally associated with cured meat. It should not be leaking foamy liquid or have a yeasty, alcoholic smell. If it does, throw it out and start over with a new batch.

If you don't want to grill all of the sausages at once, separate out what you need, tightly wrap the remainder in plastic wrap, and refrigerate for up to 1 week. For longer storage, put them into ziptop plastic bags, arranging them in a single layer, then lay the bags flat in the freezer and freeze for up to 6 months. Thaw them completely in the refrigerator before grilling.

>> CONTINUED

Prepare a medium-high fire (400° to 450°F) in a charcoal grill using the two-zone method (see page 11). When the coals are covered with white ash and the grate is hot, separate the sausage into links, if desired, and place them on the hold side of the grill. Cover and cook with the vents half-opened, turning the sausages often, until the internal temperature registers 150°F, about 20 minutes. Move the sausages to the hot side of the grill and cook uncovered, turning them almost constantly, until the internal temperature registers 165°F and the outside is golden brown, about 20 minutes. Transfer the sausage to a platter and let rest for 15 to 20 minutes.

Serve the sausages whole or cut them on a sharp diagonal into slices about ½ inch thick. Arrange some lettuce, ginger slices, chiles, peanuts, and shallots to eat along with the sausages, then enjoy. I hope you didn't forget to chill some beer in advance.

NOTE ➤——————————

Fatback is the hard fat from the under the skin of the back of a pig. You can find this important sausage ingredient at most markets selling European products.

SMOKED PORK-PEANUT SAUSAGE

⅓ cup Thai red curry paste

3 large eggs, lightly beaten

1 cup unsweetened coconut cream

¼ cup fish sauce

½ cup packed grated palm sugar or granulated coconut sugar, or ⅓ cup packed light brown sugar

1 cup unsalted roasted peanuts, finely chopped

5 pounds medium-coarse ground pork shoulder

½ cup coarsely chopped fresh cilantro leaves and stems

4 ounces natural hog casings, soaked in lukewarm water (90°F) to cover for 1 hour

¼ cup coconut oil or vegetable oil

Green lettuce, separated into individual leaves and each cut in half crosswise, for serving

6 ounces shallots, thinly sliced crosswise

3 or 4 limes, unpeeled, cut into ¼-inch cubes

10 to 12 fresh red or green bird's eye chiles, thinly sliced, for serving

This old-school central Thai sausage, *sai krok*, is traditionally served alongside a sandy, crumbly appetizer, *pla naem*, which is mainly a mix of fish flakes and ground toasted rice. (This *naem* is a different word from *naem*, the sour pork sausage reinterpreted on page 169, so don't get them confused.) Like fish and chips or bangers and mash, these two dishes are served together so routinely that it feels strange to see—or mention—one without the other. I've singled out this meatier one of the pair to feature here because I think the smoky, peanut-flecked sausage is good enough to stand on its own.

In Thailand, I smoke this sausage with coconut husks, but when I'm in Chicagoland, I prefer oak wood.

MAKES ABOUT 5 POUNDS; SERVES 6 TO 8

In a large bowl, whisk together the curry paste, eggs, coconut cream, fish sauce, and sugar, mixing well. Add the peanuts, pork, and cilantro and mix with your hands until well blended and sticky. Cook a couple of teaspoons of the mixture in a small frying pan over medium heat or in a microwave, then taste and adjust the seasoning of the mixture with more fish sauce if needed. Aim for salty first, then sweet.

Stuff the sausage meat into the casings (see page 145). Twist or tie them into 6-inch links. If you don't want to smoke all of the links at once, separate out want you need, tightly wrap the remainder in plastic wrap, and refrigerate for up to a week. For longer storage, put them into ziptop plastic bags, arranging them in a single layer, then lay the bags flat in the freezer and freeze for up to 6 months. Thaw them completely in the refrigerator before smoking.

Heat a smoker to 225°F. When the smoke runs clear, cook the sausage until the internal temperature registers 165°F, 2 to 3 hours.

Transfer the sausages to a platter, brush them on all sides with the oil, and let them rest until they are just slightly warmer than room temperature. Cut on a sharp diagonal into ½-inch-thick slices. Arrange the sausage slices on one side of a large platter; arrange the lettuce, shallots, limes, and chiles in separate mounds on the other side. To eat, put a slice of sausage on a piece of lettuce, add a few shallot pieces, a couple of lime cubes, and a couple of chile slices. Wrap into a bite-size packet and enjoy it in a single bite.

GRILLED LAO SAUSAGE

Known as *sai ua* (not to be confused with the northern Thai sausage on page 155) or as *sai kok* or *sai gok* (Lao for "sausage," equivalent to the Thai *sai krok*), this unfermented sausage features lots of fragrant herbs, with lemongrass the dominant flavor. The recipe is my take on the sausage served at my favorite Thai Lao restaurant in a Chicago suburb. They use MSG in it, which is something you can use, if you like. I've used chicken bouillon granules here to achieve a similar result.

Even though this sausage is steamed and then deep-fried at that restaurant, when you make it at home, it's much better to grill it.

MAKES ABOUT 5 POUNDS; SERVES 6 TO 8

In a bowl, combine the chiles with warm water to cover and let stand until softened, about 15 minutes. Squeeze the pieces dry and add to a small food processor. Trim off the tough outer leaves and the root end from each lemongrass stalk. Beginning from the root end, use a very sharp knife to cut each bulb into thin slices, stopping when the purple rings disappear. Add the lemongrass to the processor along with the shallots and garlic and grind to a fine—but not quite smooth—paste.

In a large bowl, combine the pork, fatback, and paste and mix well. In a small bowl, stir together the water, fish sauce, bouillon granules, and sugar until the sugar and bouillon granules dissolve, then add to the meat mixture and mix well. Add the lime leaves and green onions and knead until well blended and sticky. Cook a couple of teaspoons of the mixture in a small frying pan over medium heat or in a microwave, then taste and adjust the seasoning of the mixture if needed with more salt or sugar. The sausage should be salty and spicy and faintly sweet.

Stuff the sausage meat into the casings (see page 145). Twist or tie them into 4-inch links. If you don't want to grill all of the links at once, separate out what you need, tightly wrap the remainder in plastic wrap, and refrigerate for up to a week. For longer storage, put them into ziptop bags, arranging them in a single layer, then lay the bags flat in the freezer and freeze for up to 6 months. Thaw them completely in the refrigerator before grilling.

Prepare a medium-high fire (400° to 450°F) in a charcoal grill using the two-zone method (see page 11). When the coals are covered with white ash and the grate is hot, separate the sausage into links, if desired, and place them on the hold side of the grill. Cover and cook with the vents half-opened, turning the sausages often, until the internal temperature registers 150°F, about 20 minutes. Move the sausages to the hot side of the grill and cook uncovered, turning them almost constantly, until the internal temperature registers 165°F and the outside is golden brown, about 20 minutes. Transfer the sausage to a platter and let rest for 15 to 20 minutes.

Cut the sausage on the diagonal into ½-inch-thick slices and serve with the sticky rice.

10 large dried Thai long chiles or guajillo chiles, cut into 1-inch pieces

6 lemongrass stalks

4 ounces shallots, cubed

12 large garlic cloves

4½ pounds coarsely ground fatty pork shoulder

8 ounces fatback, finely diced (see Note, page 151)

½ cup water

¼ cup fish sauce

¼ cup chicken bouillon granules

2 tablespoons granulated sugar

¼ cup deveined and finely cut makrut lime leaves, in whisker-thin strips

4 green onions, thinly sliced

3 tablespoons coarsely ground white or black pepper

4 ounces natural hog casings, soaked in lukewarm water (90°F) to cover for 1 hour

Cooked sticky rice (see page 56), for serving

SMOKED NORTHERN THAI SAUSAGE

with Charred Green-Chile Relish

Known as *sai ua*, this popular sausage from northern Thailand is pretty easy to make, but it's important to expose it to smoke. And this is what you don't get from *sai ua* vendors at some touristy markets in Chiang Mai, the biggest and most visited city in northern Thailand, where they deep-fry their sausage instead. Smoking and grilling over a low fire of wood charcoal and coconut husks is the way to go, and you can mimic the technique in your backyard smoker. I love applewood or cherrywood chips or pellets for this.

Shrimp paste is made from salted krill, ground into a paste, and fermented. It's pungent, but a little goes a long way in providing the subtle savory taste that you expect from fermented, umami-rich ingredients. Sold in tubs, Thai-style shrimp paste, or *kapi*, works best here, and it's also the most widely available both online and at Asian stores. If you can't find it, dark miso is an acceptable substitute in this recipe.

Serve the sausage the way northern Thais do: with sticky rice lightly kneaded with your fingers into a bite-size oblong ball for scooping up some *nam phrik num*, or charred green-chile relish, another northern Thai jewel.

——————————————< **MAKES ABOUT 5 POUNDS; SERVES 6 TO 8**

In a small bowl, combine the dried chiles with warm water to cover and let stand until softened, about 15 minutes. Squeeze the pieces dry and add to a small food processor. Trim off the tough outer leaves and the root end from each lemongrass stalk. Beginning from the root end, use a very sharp knife to cut each bulb into thin slices, stopping when the purple rings disappear. Add the lemongrass to the processor along with the shallots, garlic, shrimp paste, and turmeric and grind to a fine—but not quite smooth—paste.

In a large bowl, combine the pork, fatback, and paste and mix well. Add the soy sauce, sugar, and lime leaves and knead until well blended and sticky. Cook a couple of teaspoons of the mixture in a small frying pan over medium heat or in a microwave, then taste and adjust the seasoning of the mixture, if needed, with more soy sauce or some salt.

Stuff the sausage meat into the casings (see page 145). Coil the sausage into 5- to 6-inch rounds and secure each with a bamboo skewer. Alternatively, twist or tie them into 4-inch links. If you don't want to smoke all of the links at once, separate out what you need, tightly wrap the remainder in plastic

12 large dried Thai long chiles or guajillo chiles, cut into 1-inch pieces

6 lemongrass stalks

5 ounces shallots, cubed

2 heads garlic, separated into cloves and peeled

2 tablespoons Thai shrimp paste, or ¼ cup miso or fermented soybean paste (see headnote, page 97)

1 tablespoon ground turmeric

4½ pounds coarsely ground fatty pork shoulder

8 ounces fatback, finely diced (see Note, page 151)

¼ cup soy sauce

2 teaspoons granulated sugar

¼ cup tightly packed deveined and finely cut makrut lime leaves, in whisker-thin strips

Salt (optional)

4 ounces natural hog casings, soaked in lukewarm water (90°F) to cover for 1 hour

RELISH

2 heads garlic, separated into cloves and peeled

3 large shallots, about 1 ounce each, peeled

8 ounces green finger hot chiles, stemmed

8 ounces green Anaheim chiles, stemmed

1 tablespoon fish sauce

Salt

Cooked sticky rice (see page 56), for serving

>> CONTINUED

wrap, and refrigerate for up to a week. For longer storage, put them into ziptop plastic bags, arranging them in a single layer, then lay the bags flat in the freezer and freeze for up to 6 months. Thaw them completely in the refrigerator before smoking.

Set a smoker to 225°F. When the smoker reaches the target temperature and the smoke runs clear, place the sausages on the grate and cook until the internal temperature registers 165°F, 2 to 3 hours. Remove from the smoker and let rest for 15 minutes before slicing.

While the sausages are smoking, make the relish: Soak five or six 12-inch bamboo skewers in water to cover for 1 to 2 hours. Light a full chimney of charcoal. When the coals are ready, spread them out on the bottom of a small kettle grill or a hibachi for cooking over a high fire.

Thread the garlic, shallots, and chiles onto the soaked skewers. When the coals are covered with white ash and the grate is hot, grill the relish ingredients, rolling and flipping them almost constantly, until softened and charred, about 8 minutes.

Remove from the grill and let cool completely. Slide the garlic, shallots, and chiles off the skewers into a mortar (preferable) or small food processor (okay but be careful not to overgrind) and grind to a chunky paste. Transfer to a medium bowl and stir in the fish sauce, then taste and adjust the seasoning with salt if needed. The relish should be salty and spicy.

Serve the sausages with the sticky rice and the relish.

BEEF & LAMB

"HEAVENLY" RACKS OF LAMB

Lamb is not cooked as often as other types of meat in Southeast Asia. In Thailand, lamb consumption has largely been limited to the Muslim communities and, more recently, to high-end Western and fusion restaurants and to hotpot establishments. While young urban Southeast Asians have slowly grown to like and even crave the taste of lamb, the general sentiment is still that it's intolerably gamy.

My exposure to—and appreciation for—nonmainstream meats, such as lamb, mutton, and goat, began in early childhood in Bangkok. My mother would drive across the city to a market in Bang Rak, a multicultural neighborhood, just to buy mutton and goat from a halal butcher for her cooking experiments. Her most successful effort was a spin-off of the classic deep-fried beef jerky known as *nuea sawan* (literally "heavenly beef" or "beef from heaven"). Instead of the traditional thin slices or strips of beef, she used racks of mutton ribs and grilled them whole over a pile of coconut husks and wood charcoal. It was a big hit, even among the older relatives who had sworn they'd never touch "that thing."

SERVES 6 TO 8

4 whole racks of lamb, 2 to 2½ pounds each, membrane removed, bones frenched, and fat cap left on

2 teaspoons salt

3 teaspoons ground white or black pepper

2 tablespoons fish sauce

3 tablespoons tamarind paste (see Note, page 23)

¼ cup packed grated palm sugar or granulated coconut sugar, or 3 tablespoons packed light brown sugar

¼ cup coriander seeds, coarsely cracked

2 teaspoons toasted white sesame seeds

¼ cup vegetable oil

Cooked jasmine rice, for serving

Using the tip of a knife, make slits in a crosshatch pattern on the fat cap of each lamb rack, spacing them about ¾ inch apart and cutting through the cap but not into the meat. In a small bowl, stir together the salt, pepper, fish sauce, and tamarind. Rub the mixture all over the lamb racks, pushing it down into the slits. Cover and chill for 6 to 8 hours.

The the lamb racks out of the refrigerator. Stir together the sugar, coriander seeds, sesame seeds, and vegetable oil. Rub the mixture all over the lamb racks, concentrating on the scored fat caps and pushing it down into the slits. Leave the lamb racks to rest at room temperature for 30 minutes.

Prepare a medium-high fire (400° to 450°F) in a charcoal grill using the two-zone method (see page 11). When the coals are covered with white ash and the grate is hot, place the racks, fat side down, in the middle of the grill, between the hot and hold sides. Cover and cook until the fat sides are nicely browned, 5 to 6 minutes. Turn the racks over and move them to the hold side of the grill. Re-cover and cook with the vents half-opened, until the internal temperature in the center of the meat away from bone registers 130°F for medium-rare, 15 to 20 minutes. Transfer the racks, meat side up, to one or more sheet pans and let rest for 15 minutes.

Cut the racks into chops, trying to keep the crust top intact, and arrange on a platter. Serve with the rice.

CAVEMAN-STYLE REVERSE-SEARED RIB-EYE STEAKS

with *Spicy Grape Salad*

STEAKS

4 bone-in rib-eye steaks, 1½ to 2 inches thick

1½ tablespoons coarse sea salt or kosher salt, plus a small pinch for finishing

SALAD

3 cups seedless red or green grapes

3 large garlic cloves, pressed or minced

3 or 4 fresh bird's eye chiles, minced

4 fresh mint stems stripped of leaves, minced

1 tablespoon fish sauce

2 tablespoons fresh lime juice

1 teaspoon granulated sugar

⅓ cup fresh mint leaves, for garnish

Cooked jasmine rice, for serving

As a child, I watched with great curiosity the way every cook in my family instinctively knew how to throw edibles onto a heap of coals and then bring them out in the form of one delicious dish after another. Cooking directly on top of the fire is often referred to as caveman-style grilling or "dirty" grilling, but in my household, such cooking has never been a novelty. Instead, it has been a way of maximizing the coals at every stage.

When the coals are hot and glowing, large, hardy river prawns, for example, are roasted directly on them. When the coals are thoroughly covered in thick layers of ash and about to die out, the ash is fanned away with a woven bamboo fan—an essential tool in every household with a clay charcoal grill—and large cuts of meat or small whole fish are placed directly on them. When they have become even more ash laden and the temperature has dropped way down, eggplants, fresh and dried chiles, shallots, or whole heads of garlic are buried in the embers, later to emerge ready to be turned into various relishes and sauces.

For this recipe, I cook the steaks with the reverse-searing method, which I learned from J. Kenji López-Alt, author of *The Food Lab: Better Home Cooking Through Science*. It's the least complicated and most foolproof way to cook a thick piece of bone-in steak without ruining it. It calls for cooking the steaks at a low temperature and then searing them over very high heat to char and crisp the outside. In this case, I've taken it a step further by cooking the steak right on top of the burning coals.

The grape salad is an adaptation of the recipe that Vichit Mukura, former executive chef of the Mandarin Oriental Bangkok, shared with me when I interviewed him in 2014. In Mukura's recipe, you mix chunks of grilled steak with grapes for a main-dish salad. I like to serve them separately, so the crust on the steaks remains crisp and smoky.

⟨ SERVES 4

To prep the steaks: Sprinkle the meaty surfaces evenly with the salt. Set a large wire rack on a sheet pan and put the steaks on the rack. Refrigerate, uncovered, for 8 to 10 hours.

≫ CONTINUED

Position a rack in the middle of the oven and preheat the oven to 220°F. Place the steaks—still on the rack on the sheet pan—in the oven and cook, checking often, until the internal temperature registers your preferred doneness: 115° to 120°F for rare, 125°F for medium-rare, 130°F for medium, 140° to 145°F for medium-well, and 150° to 155°F for well done. The timing will range from about 20 minutes for rare to about 45 minutes for well done.

Meanwhile, prep the salad: Combine the grapes, garlic, chiles, mint, fish sauce, lime juice, and sugar in a medium bowl but do not toss them yet. Cover and refrigerate.

When the steaks are almost ready, light a full chimney of charcoal. When the coals are ready, spread them out on the bottom of a kettle grill for cooking over a hot fire.

Meanwhile, quickly toss the salad and then taste to see if you like it. The result will depend on how sweet or sour your grapes are, so experiment, adding more lime juice and sugar or even fish sauce to achieve a salad that is equally sweet, sour, and salty. Cover and refrigerate until serving.

Take the steaks out of the oven and blot all of the surfaces dry with paper towels. Fan the ash off the coals with a piece of cardboard, and immediately place the steaks directly on the coals. Working attentively and watching the steaks closely, use a long pair of tongs to flip the steaks, to turn them, to move them around, and to hold them sideways to brown them thoroughly on all sides. You have to keep the steaks moving because the fat will create flare-ups and the intense heat can turn a beautifully charred steak into a burnt steak in seconds if you're not paying attention. Once the steaks are thoroughly charred and have formed a golden crust, which should take 1 to 2 minutes, remove them from the coals.

Brush any ash off the steaks. Serve them whole or slice them against the grain, arrange on individual plates, and crumble a small pinch of sea salt over them. Spoon the grape salad alongside the meat, then scatter the mint leaves over the salad. Serve immediately with the rice.

GRILLED SKIRT STEAKS

with Spicy Roasted Tomato Sauce

STEAKS

¼ cup vegetable oil

2 tablespoons soy sauce

2 tablespoons oyster sauce

2 teaspoons ground white
or black pepper

3 pounds skirt steaks

1 tablespoon of Thai glutinous
rice (see headnote, page 56)

SAUCE

6 ounces cherry tomatoes

1½ ounces shallots, halved

5 large garlic cloves

1 tablespoon fish sauce

2 tablespoons fresh lime juice

3 tablespoons red pepper
flakes

1 teaspoon packed light
brown sugar

¼ cup coarsely chopped
fresh cilantro leaves and
stems

Handful of fresh cilantro
leaves, for garnish

Cooked sticky rice,
(see page 56) for serving

Although people around the world eat many of the same animals, each culture has its own preference for how to butcher the animal, what parts to eat, and how best to cut the meat to accommodate local cooking styles. When I travel to different countries, I always make time to survey the meat department of a local supermarket. It's a window into another culinary culture.

Here's a case in point: While skin-on oxtails, beef tendon, and beef drop flank are common throughout Southeast Asia, skirt steak, arguably the beefiest cut on the entire cow and a cut that can be found anywhere in North America, is not. I didn't realize this was part of a cow until I came to the United States for school many years ago. To say I fell in love with the taste is an understatement. And the relatively low cost of the cut was kind to my meager student income. I even went through a phase during which I used skirt steak to make nearly every Thai dish I had eaten while growing up, even shoehorning it into ones that shouldn't be made with skirt steak.

This adaptation of the classic grilled beef dish *suea ronghai* (crying tiger) works very well. No shoehorning here. Skirt steaks tend to buckle, so have a heavy burger press or a brick covered with foil handy to press them down, which also helps with the caramelization.

⟨ **SERVES 4**

To prep the steaks: In a large bowl, whisk together the oil, soy sauce, oyster sauce, and pepper. Add the steaks and turn to coat them evenly with the oil mixture. Cover and refrigerate for 4 to 6 hours.

Soak five or six 12-inch bamboo skewers in water to cover for 1 to 2 hours.

Meanwhile, put the rice in a dry, small frying pan and toast over medium-low heat, stirring almost constantly, until the grains are golden brown and have a nutty aroma, about 15 minutes. Immediately transfer the rice to a small heatproof bowl and let cool completely (do not leave it in the pan, as it will continue to toast). In a small food processor or a mortar, grind the rice to a coarse powder, then set aside.

Prepare a medium-high fire (400° to 450°F) in a charcoal grill using the two-zone method (see page 11).

>> CONTINUED

To make the sauce: Thread the tomatoes, shallot halves, and garlic onto the soaked skewers, keeping each ingredient on its own skewer or skewers. When the coals are covered with white ash and the grate is hot, place the skewers in the middle of the grill halfway between the hot side and the hold side and cook uncovered, turning frequently, until charred and softened, 8 to 10 minutes. Transfer to a plate and cool completely.

While the skewers are cooling, place the steaks on the grill near the hot side and cook uncovered, turning once and pressing down with a burger press or a brick covered with aluminum foil to prevent buckling, until well caramelized on both sides, 5 to 7 minutes per side. Transfer to a cutting board and tent with foil.

Working quickly, put the tomatoes, shallots, and garlic into a food processor and process to a coarse paste. Transfer to a medium bowl and stir in the fish sauce, lime juice, pepper flakes, sugar, and cilantro. The sauce should have the consistency of a chunky salsa. Taste and adjust the seasoning with more lime juice, fish sauce, and pepper flakes, if needed. The sauce should taste primarily sour and spicy and then salty, with a little bit of sweet.

Cut the steaks along the grain into 3-inch-thick strips, then slice each strip against the grain into 1/2-inch-thick slices. Arrange on a serving platter, sprinkle with the ground toasted rice, and garnish with the cilantro. Put the sauce in a separate bowl and serve alongside, accompanied with the cooked sticky rice

SMOKED FERMENTED SHORT RIBS

This dish is my own unconventional riff on the northeastern Thai soured pork called *naem* in all regions of Thailand, *jin som* in northern Thailand, *som mu* in Laos, and *nem chua* in Vietnam.

In its traditional form, *naem* has the appearance of loosely pressed ham, and it is routinely served raw as an accompaniment to beer or whiskey and soda or is used as an ingredient in such dishes as fried rice and salads. You'll also often find *naem* packed into a cylinder, about 2 inches across and 4 inches long, and grilled on a bamboo skewer.

Although coarsely ground pork is the default meat of choice for *naem*, a version made with coarsely ground beef is found in some Thai Muslim communities. Pork rib tips have also gained popularity in the last couple of decades, as have chicken knee joints (they're delicious). People who don't eat meat have even taken to making *naem* with mushrooms.

Over the years, I have experimented making *naem* with several different meats, but the fermentation process stays the same: sticky rice is used as the fermentation agent that provides sugar to the bacteria in order to create lactic acid and salt, which both flavor the sausage and prevent the development of bad bacteria. Of all the meats I have tried, beef short ribs, a cut I particularly like, have yielded my favorite iteration.

Cleanliness is key whenever you make a recipe that involves fermentation. Make sure everything that touches the meat is immaculately clean. If the garlic has even just the tiniest bit of mold on it, don't use it. Do not be tempted to reduce the amount of salt, as salt helps inhibit undesirable bacteria, so you need the amount specified.

I use milder woods for smoking soured short ribs than I do for the pork sausage. A strong wood such as mesquite is overpowering. I quite like maple and cherry.

6 pounds bone-in beef short ribs, trimmed of the papery membrane and cut into individual ribs

4 heads garlic, cloves separated, peeled, rinsed well, and dried thoroughly

2¼ cups packed cooked sticky rice (see page 56) or long-grain rice

¼ cup plus 1 tablespoon kosher salt

1 level teaspoon pink curing salt #1 (see Note, page 170)

½ cup room-temperature water

½ cup vegetable oil

¼ cup freshly ground black peppercorns

1 cup no-salt-added beef or chicken stock, in a spray bottle

Cooked sticky rice (see page 56) or jasmine rice, for serving

———————————————⟨ **MAKES ABOUT 5 POUNDS; SERVES 6 TO 8**

Rinse the ribs and dry them thoroughly with paper towels. Put them into a very clean, large bowl. In a food processor, combine the garlic, rice, and salt and blend to a somewhat smooth paste. Scrape every last bit of the paste

>> CONTINUED

into the bowl with the ribs; don't mix just yet. Dissolve the curing salt in the water and add to the bowl. With gloved or immaculately clean hands, mix everything together, doing your best to keep each rib intact and to coat each rib thoroughly with the rice mixture.

Transfer the ribs to one large or two medium vacuum sealer storage bags and seal closed. If you don't have a vacuum sealer, you will need to sterilize one or more jars with tight-fitting lids. A jar must be just large enough to accommodate the tightly packed ribs, with no gaps between the ribs or between the ribs and the lid. The idea is to eliminate as much air as possible. Put the ribs into the jar and pack them down tightly until they are about ¼ inch *above* the rim, then push down firmly as you screw on the lid.

Leave the vacuum-sealed or jarred ribs at room temperature (70° to 75°F) for 4 days.

To cook the ribs, set a smoker to 225°F. Rinse the paste off the ribs and pat them dry. Rub the oil all over the ribs, followed by the pepper. When the smoker reaches the target temperature and the smoke runs clear, arrange the ribs, bone side down, on the grate and close the lid. Smoke the ribs, spritzing them with the stock every hour, until the internal temperature in the center of a rib away from the bone registers 200° to 205°F, 7 to 8 hours.

Remove the ribs from the smoker and serve immediately with the rice.

NOTE >————————————

The option of using pink curing salt is included here for your safety, following the guidelines of the National Center for Home Food Preservation.

GRILLED BEEF SKEWERS

I love how this Cambodian grilled beef, known as *sach ko jakak*, doesn't need to be dipped into a sauce to taste great. The herbaceous spice paste in the marinade—what the Cambodians call *kroeung*—has all the flavors you need. This is what I like most about Cambodian food: the dishes aren't usually spicy, but they have complex, fresh, vibrant flavors and the ingredients are allowed to shine.

This recipe comes from a friend of mine, Bussaba, a Cambodian who lives in Surin Province in Thailand. This is how her mother used to make it for her and her siblings when they were growing up.

SERVES 4

Trim off the tough outer leaves and the root end from each lemongrass stalk. Beginning from the root end, use a very sharp knife to cut each bulb into thin slices, stopping when the purple rings disappear. In a small food processor, combine the lemongrass, garlic, ginger, turmeric, and oil and blend to a fine—but not too smooth—paste. Scrape into a large bowl, add the oyster sauce, fish sauce, and sugar, and stir well. Add the beef and mix until evenly coated. Cover and refrigerate for at least 6 hours or up to overnight.

Soak eight 12-inch bamboo skewers in water to cover for 1 to 2 hours.

Light a full chimney of charcoal. When the coals are ready, spread them out on the bottom of a hibachi (preferable) or kettle grill for cooking over a medium-high fire (400° to 450°F).

Thread the beef onto the soaked skewers (see page 93). When the coals are covered with white ash and the grate is hot, grill the beef, turning frequently, until charred on the edges with no pink remaining, about 10 minutes.

Remove from the grill and serve immediately with the rice.

6 lemongrass stalks

8 large garlic cloves

Thumb-size piece fresh ginger, cubed

2 teaspoons ground turmeric

½ cup vegetable oil

¼ cup oyster sauce

1 tablespoon fish sauce

1 tablespoon granulated sugar

2 pounds chuck or sirloin steak or beef tenderloin, cut against the grain into thin, bite-size pieces

Cooked jasmine rice, for serving

PHANAENG-CURRY BEEF SKEWERS

with Grilled Pumpkin

One reason *phanaeng* curry is one of the most beloved in Thailand is that, when traditionally made, it's thicker and more concentrated than most other curries. Each spoonful packs more flavors—but not more heat—than any other curry. Like the other Thai curries, *phanaeng* is served in a bowl, to be eaten with rice. But my entire extended family watched with amazement as a caterer at my grandfather's seventy-second birthday party threaded beef, marinated in curry paste, onto the blades of coconut leaves that had been trimmed down to their slender but sturdy midrib, creating skewers. He grilled the meat along with large cubes of pumpkin skewered the same way. (This was long before serving traditional dishes deconstructed became a thing.) That party was full of great food, but this is the only dish most of us still remember. In fact, we have been making our reverse-engineered version—what you're looking at here—at every family reunion since that day.

You can serve these skewers with cooked jasmine rice. If you do, season the sauce with a heavier hand to balance the bland rice. Be sure to use a well-marbled, quick-cooking cut of beef, such as rib-eye or sirloin steak. The pumpkin or winter squash should be dense and low in moisture. Kabocha, Buttercup, Musquée de Provence (aka Fairy Tale pumpkin), and Potimarron squash (aka Red Kuri) are my absolute favorites. When I can't find any of these, I use common butternut squash, which is not too shabby. The *phanaeng* (also spelled *panang*) curry paste is sold in tubs (Nittaya or Mae Ploy is a good brand) in Southeast Asian markets.

SERVES 6

To prep the beef: In a large bowl, stir together the curry paste, peanut butter, sugar, coconut milk, and salt, mixing well. Add the beef and stir to coat evenly. Cover and refrigerate for 2 hours.

Soak twelve 12-inch bamboo skewers in water to cover for 1 to 2 hours.

To prep the pumpkin: About 15 minutes before the beef is done marinating, fill a 4-quart saucepan half full with water and bring to a boil. Pour the ice-cold water into a large bowl and put the bowl into the sink. Add the pumpkin cubes to the boiling water and blanch for 1 minute. Using a fine-mesh skimmer, quickly transfer the pumpkin to the cold water to stop the cooking. Drain the pumpkin, pat dry, and transfer to a medium bowl. Add the salt and mix gently but thoroughly; set aside.

>> CONTINUED

BEEF

2 tablespoons packed phanaeng curry paste (see headnote) or red curry paste

2 heaping tablespoons unsweetened natural creamy peanut butter

2 tablespoons packed grated palm sugar or granulated coconut sugar, or 1 tablespoon packed light brown sugar

¾ cup unsweetened full-fat coconut milk

1 teaspoon salt

2 pounds well-marbled rib-eye steaks or sirloin steak or tips, cut against the grain into bite-size pieces about ¼ inch thick

PUMPKIN

8 cups ice-cold water

2 pounds dense, low-moisture pumpkin or winter squash (see headnote), peeled, seeded, and cut into 1-inch cubes

¼ teaspoon salt

SAUCE

2 tablespoons coconut oil

2 tablespoons packed phanaeng curry paste or red curry paste

1½ cups unsweetened full-fat coconut milk

1 tablespoon packed grated palm sugar or granulated coconut sugar, or 2 teaspoons packed light brown sugar

2 teaspoons fish sauce

½ to ¾ cup coconut oil, melted, for brushing

½ cup unsalted roasted peanuts, coarsely chopped, for garnish

4 to 6 fresh red bird's eye chiles, or 2 larger hot red chiles, thinly sliced, for garnish

5 or 6 makrut lime leaves, deveined and cut into whisker-thin strips, or ½ cup fresh Thai basil leaves, for garnish

Divide the beef into twelve equal portions; do the same with the pumpkin. Working with one portion of beef and one of pumpkin, alternately thread them onto a soaked skewer (see page 93). Push the beef and pumpkin snugly against one another to form a compact bundle toward the tip end of the skewer, leaving the blunt end bare to use as a handle. Repeat with the remaining meat and pumpkin portions and skewers.

Prepare a medium-high fire (400° to 450°F) in a charcoal grill using the two-zone method (see page 11). Alternatively, light a full chimney of charcoal, and when the coals are ready, spread them out on the bottom of a hibachi for cooking over a medium fire (350° to 375°F).

While waiting for the grill to heat, make the sauce: In a 1-quart saucepan, combine the oil and curry paste over medium-high heat. When the oil has melted, stir until fragrant, about 1 minute. Add the coconut milk and sugar and simmer for 3 minutes, stirring often. Add the fish sauce, then taste and adjust the seasoning with more fish sauce if needed. Keep warm.

When the coals are covered with white ash and the grate is hot, place the skewers in the middle of the grill halfway between the hot side and the hold side. Cook uncovered, brushing with the oil and flipping and turning the skewers as needed to cook evenly, until both the beef and the pumpkin are lightly charred, 10 to 12 minutes.

Transfer the skewers to a large platter. Drizzle the warm sauce over them and sprinkle with the peanuts first, followed by the chiles, and then the lime leaves. If using basil leaves, tear them into small pieces at the last minute. Serve immediately.

GREEN CURRY BEEF SKEWERS

with Fried Basil Oil

4 pounds boneless rib-eye steak, beef tenderloin, or boneless leg of lamb, cut against the grain into bite-size pieces

1 cup green curry paste

½ cup packed grated palm sugar or granulated coconut sugar, or ⅓ cup packed light brown sugar

2 tablespoons fish sauce

1 cup vegetable oil

Pinkie-size piece fresh turmeric root, halved lengthwise (optional)

1½ cups fresh Thai or common basil leaves

Cooked jasmine rice, for serving

Although green curry paste goes well with all types of meat, it brings out the best in red meat. I use beef here, but just as often I use boneless lamb from the leg. The basil oil is a finishing touch that perfumes the dish with the scent of Thai basil and provides richness. I call for quite a lot of curry paste here, but feel free to adjust the amount to suit your taste. Those who want it really hot may want to add more, but keep in mind that you will be introducing more salt to the dish, too, as commercial curry pastes tend to be salty. Look for a brand imported from Thailand, such as Mae Ploy or Nittaya.

Lightly misting the basil leaves with water before you drop them in the hot oil will create crispy leaves that are vibrantly green—almost like stained glass—as opposed to dark brownish green.

SERVES 8

In a large bowl, combine the beef, curry paste, sugar, and fish sauce and mix well. Cover and refrigerate for at least 8 hours or up overnight.

Soak twenty-four 6-inch bamboo skewers in water to cover for 1 to 2 hours.

Cook a couple of pieces of beef in a small frying pan over medium heat or in a microwave, then taste them and adjust the seasoning with more fish sauce and sugar if needed, keeping in mind that the accompanying rice will be bland. The meat should taste salty and then a little sweet.

Divide the beef into twelve equal portions. Thread each portion onto a skewer (see page 93).

Put the basil leaves in a small bowl and lightly mist them with water. Line a small plate with a paper towel. Place the bowl of basil, the towel-lined plate, and a small saucepan with a heatproof handle near the grill. Keep the leaves lightly misted. The moisture helps the leaves turn a bright, beautiful jewel-like green when they are fried. (Don't overdo it, though, as the moisture can also cause splattering.)

Prepare a medium-high fire (400° to 450°F) in a charcoal grill using the two-zone method (see page 11). Place the skewers on the hot side of the grill and cook with the lid off until you get some charring on the outside,

>> CONTINUED

5 to 7 minutes. Move the skewers to the hold side of the grill, cover, and cook with the vents half-opened until no pink is visible in the beef, about 10 minutes.

About 5 minutes before the meat is done, in the reserved frying pan, combine the oil and turmeric (if using) and place it on the hot side of the grill. When the turmeric sizzles and the oil is turning yellow and is hot, drop 1 cup of the basil leaves into the oil and stand back. Within seconds the basil leaves will be crisp. Using a mesh skimmer, transfer them to the towel-lined plate and remove the pan from the grill.

To serve, transfer the skewers to a large platter. Drizzle some of the turmeric- and basil-infused oil over the beef. Top with the fried basil leaves and the remaining ½ cup fresh leaves. Serve immediately with the rice.

GRILLED STUFFED LEMONGRASS

In the grilling repertoire of Southeast Asia, there are a few dishes in which seasoned ground meat is formed, kebab-style, on lemongrass stalks, using the herb as skewers. The most brilliant of them, in my opinion, is this classic Lao dish, *ua si kai*, in which the meat, rather than being wrapped around the stalks, is embedded in them.

What makes a tremendous difference is that each lemongrass stalk is partially split at its bulbous end—the part where the highest concentration of essential oil resides—forming a "cage," or woven basket of sorts, that holds the sausage meat in place. A stalk that has been cut or bruised releases its perfume more effectively than an intact stalk.

This leads me to my next point: To eat this dish, I recommend picking up a lemongrass stalk with your hand and attacking it with your teeth, like a shark. The lemongrass is not meant to be eaten, and it's too fibrous for you to inadvertently chew through it. But because the lemongrass will release its essential oil as you crush it with your teeth, you will get a burst of lemongrass fragrance with each bite. If this is too uncouth for company, I'd lose the company.

This grilled version of *ua si kai* is my adaptation of the recipe from *Traditional Recipes of Laos* by Phia Sing, who served in the royal palace in Luang Prabang in the early 1900s. The original recipe has you coat the stuffed lemongrass stalks with beaten egg and deep-fry them, and it yields spectacular results. However, I've found that the scent of lemongrass comes through more clearly when the lemongrass is grilled.

Use the most voluptuous lemongrass stalks you can find. An Asian market with a lush produce department is your best bet.

1½ pounds ground beef sirloin

4 green onions, finely chopped

6 large garlic cloves, minced

2 tablespoons cornstarch

2 tablespoons fish sauce

1 teaspoon salt

2 teaspoons ground white or black pepper

1 large egg white

20 to 24 fat lemongrass stalks

½ cup vegetable or coconut oil, melted

———————————————⟨ **SERVES 4 AS AN APPETIZER**

In a medium bowl, combine the beef, green onions, garlic, cornstarch, fish sauce, salt, pepper, and egg white and knead with your hand until the mixture is sticky. Cover and refrigerate for 2 to 4 hours.

Remove the tough, spotty outer leaves of each lemongrass stalk. Trim them so they are 6 inches in length, measuring from the root end. Working in small batches, wrap the stalks loosely with two or three layers of damp paper towels and microwave on high until they are just softened and pliable, 1½ to 2 minutes. Using the tip of a sharp paring knife, and starting about ½ inch

⟩⟩ **CONTINUED**

from the root end, make several lengthwise cuts all the way through, each 4 inches long, around each bulb.

Divide the meat into twenty to twenty-four equal portions, depending on the number of stalks, and form each portion into a compact elongated ball. Stuff one portion of the meat into each lemongrass bulb, trying to get the meat to stay inside the "cage" as best as you can (if some oozes out, don't worry too much). Once you have filled all of the lemongrass bulbs, moisten your hands and press each filled bulb between your palms to form a football-shaped capsule, with the meat securely inside the cage.

Light a full chimney of charcoal. When the coals are ready, spread them out on the bottom of a hibachi grill for cooking over a medium fire (350° to 375°F).

When the coals are covered with white ash and the grate is hot, grill the stuffed lemongrass, turning the stalks often and brushing along the way with the oil, until no pink remains, the lemongrass is lightly charred, and the sausage meat holds its shape when you squeeze the lemongrass bulb lightly, 7 to 10 minutes.

Transfer the lemongrass to a large platter and serve slightly warmer than room temperature.

SALADS, SNACKS & SWEETS

GRILLED EGGPLANT SALAD

In Southeast Asia, long, slender, light green eggplants are the most common variety and are the best choice for this recipe. They require little preparation, don't need to be salted to extract bitterness, and don't even need to be peeled. Just throw them on the grill whole and cook them until they are charred on the outside and soft and sweet on the inside—a perfect canvas on which to paint a colorful combination of flavors and textures. The coconut milk–based dressing used here reinforces the creaminess of the grilled eggplants, while the crisp shallots and crunchy cashews provide contrasting texture. There's so much flavor in this satisfying dish that guests may not even notice that *yam ma-khuea yao* is meat-free.

In the West, purple Japanese eggplants are the perfect substitute for Thai long, green ones, which aren't available in most areas.

SERVES 4

Line a small plate with a paper towel. In a small frying pan, combine the oil and shallots, place over medium heat, and cook, stirring often, until the shallots are crisp and golden brown, 7 to 10 minutes. Using a slotted spoon, transfer the shallots to the towel-lined plate and let cool. Reserve the shallot oil for another use.

Light a chimney full of charcoal. When the coals are ready, spread them out on the bottom of a hibachi or small kettle grill for cooking over medium fire (350°F).

Meanwhile, make the dressing: In a 1-quart saucepan, whisk together the coconut milk and cornstarch, then place over medium heat and bring to a boil, whisking constantly. Lower the heat and simmer for 2 minutes. Remove from the heat and let cool to lukewarm. Stir in the lime juice and sugar, then taste and add salt. Aim for a dressing that's equally sour, sweet, and salty. Set aside.

When the coals are covered with white ash and the grate is hot, grill the eggplant all over, flipping them as needed, until charred and a fork slid into the flesh meets no resistance. Transfer to a cutting board.

When the eggplants are cool enough to handle, cut them crosswise into 1-inch-thick pieces and arrange the pieces on a platter. Drizzle the pieces with the dressing and sprinkle with the crisp shallots, followed by the pepper flakes, cashews, and cilantro. Sprinkle the mint leaves over the top. Serve immediately with the rice.

¾ cup vegetable oil

2 ounces shallots, halved lengthwise, then thinly sliced lengthwise

1½ cups unsweetened full-fat coconut milk

2 tablespoons cornstarch

¼ cup fresh lime juice

1½ teaspoons granulated sugar

Salt

6 Thai long, green, or Japanese purple eggplants (no substitutes), halved lengthwise

1 tablespoon red pepper flakes

½ cup unsalted roasted cashews, coarsely chopped

¼ cup coarsely chopped fresh cilantro leaves and stems

¼ cup fresh mint leaves

Cooked jasmine rice, for serving

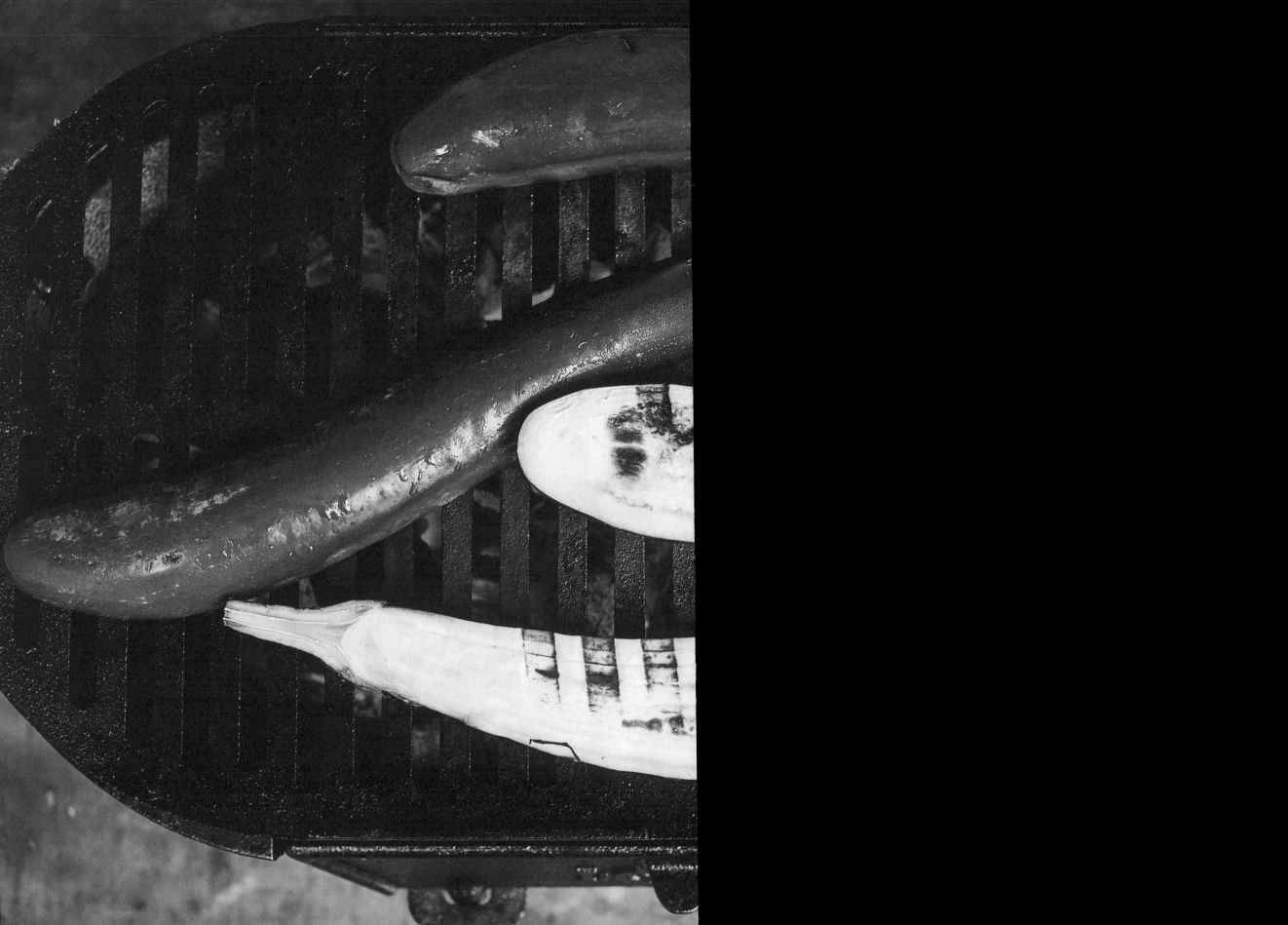

GRILLED MIXED MUSHROOM SALAD

2 tablespoons Thai glutinous rice (see headnote, page 56) or long-grain rice

3 tablespoons vegetable oil

½ cup unsalted roasted cashew halves

4 pounds (they shrink!) assorted mushrooms, trimmed

¼ cup fresh lime juice

2 tablespoons fish sauce

1 teaspoon granulated sugar

2 teaspoons dried red pepper flakes

2 ounces shallots, halved lengthwise then thinly sliced lengthwise

As many bird's eye chiles (or any hot chiles) as you like, cut into thin slices

½ cup coarsely chopped cilantro leaves and stems

½ cup mint leaves

Cooked jasmine rice, for serving

Use many types of mushrooms in this salad to get in as many textures as you can. Include ones that are more delicate like oyster mushrooms and hearty, meaty mushrooms like king oyster mushrooms (*Pleurotus eryngii*), which can be found at any Korean or Japanese market. Smaller mushrooms like hon shimeji or white beech are great, too.

SERVES 4

Put the rice in a small frying pan and toast over medium heat, stirring almost constantly until the grains are golden brown and have a nutty aroma. Immediately transfer them to a heatproof bowl to cool completely (don't leave them in the pan to cool). Grind into coarse powder; set aside. Wipe the pan clean, add the vegetable oil to it along with the cashews. Put the pan on medium heat and gently heat both the oil and the cashews together, stirring constantly, until the cashews are golden brown, 3 to 4 minutes. Transfer to a towel-lined plate to drain.

Light a chimney full of charcoal. When the coals are ready, spread them onto the bottom of a hibachi or small kettle grill for cooking over a medium fire (350° to 375°F). When the coals are covered with white hot ash and the grate is hot, grill the mushrooms, flipping them as needed, until wilted and lightly charred. Use your judgment as to how. For some smaller mushrooms, you should grill them on skewers; for some larger mushrooms, such as king oyster mushrooms or large oyster mushrooms, you can slice them first (to increase the surface area) before placing them directly on the grill grate.

Cut the mushrooms into bite-size pieces and place in a mixing bowl. Add half of the ground toasted rice, the lime juice, fish sauce, sugar, and pepper flakes. Mix well and taste to see if you need more fish sauce or lime juice (the salad should be sour first, then salty, then a little bit sweet). Fold in the shallots, chiles, and cilantro; mix well. Transfer to a serving platter. Top with the remaining ground rice, cashews, and mint leaves. Serve immediately with rice.

GRILLED CORN
with Coconut Sauce

I'm drawn to food that straddles the worlds of savory and sweet—something that could be either but is committed to neither. And this is why *pot ang* is my favorite street snack when I'm in Cambodia. Grilled corn is already good on its own, but what makes *pot ang* special is the coconut sauce that coats it. The velvety sauce is mildly sweet and just as mildly salty. The pièces de résistance are the green onion specks stirred in at the last minute—simple and sublime.

For the best result, use the finely milled rice flour sold at every Asian grocery store. Make sure you use the type made from long-grain rice rather than glutinous rice. The package will be labeled simply "rice flour," not "glutinous rice flour" or "sweet rice flour." Erawan is a great brand. You can use glutinous rice flour, or even tapioca starch or cornstarch, in this recipe, but I've found that anything other than long-grain rice flour turns the coconut sauce a bit slimy.

1½ cups unsweetened full-fat coconut milk

2 tablespoons rice flour

3 tablespoons packed grated palm sugar or granulated coconut sugar, or 2 tablespoons packed light brown sugar

½ teaspoon salt

6 ears corn in their husks

¼ cup thinly sliced green onions

SERVES 6

In a 1-quart saucepan, whisk together the coconut milk and rice flour until no lumps remain. Put the pan over medium heat and bring to a boil, stirring occasionally. Lower the heat and simmer until the sauce is velvety, like a light gravy, 1 to 2 minutes. Add the sugar and salt and stir until dissolved. Taste and add more sugar or salt if needed. Remove from the heat.

Prepare a medium-high fire (400° to 450°F) in a charcoal grill using the two-zone method (see page 11). When the coals are covered with white ash and the grate is hot, place the corn, still in the husk, on the hold side of the grill. Cover and cook, turning the ears a couple of times, for 10 minutes.

Remove the corn from the grill and carefully pull back the husks on each ear, exposing all of the kernels and leaving husks attached to the stem. Remove and discard the silk. Tie the husks in place with kitchen string. It should look like you're giving each ear of corn a ponytail.

Put the corn back on the grill halfway between the hold side and the hot side and cook, moving and turning them as needed, until they are browned on all sides, about 6 minutes.

Arrange the corn on a serving platter and let to cool until slightly warmer than room temperature. Stir the green onions into the coconut sauce, then spoon the sauce over the corn, making sure the corn is well coated. Serve immediately.

GRILLED EGGS IN BANANA-LEAF BOATS

8 (7 by 10-inch) pieces
banana leaf

8 large eggs, lightly beaten

½ cup water

½ cup shrimp meat,
finely diced

2 Chinese chive stalks or
green onions, sliced ⅛ inch
thick, plus more for garnish

4 fresh red bird's eye chiles,
thinly sliced, plus more for
garnish

1 teaspoon salt

The hardest physical thing I have ever done in my life was a monthlong volunteer trip our high school class took to the remotest parts of rural Mae Hong Son, where the north of Thailand meets Myanmar. There were no roads in the area, so we had to travel on foot. The goal was to promote dental hygiene among the local children, who had no idea what a toothbrush was. Hiking up the steep hills on unbeaten paths was difficult enough, but we also had to carry five-gallon bottles of drinking water and a large, heavy generator. Although I had youth on my side at the time, the physical and mental exhaustion was almost too much to bear. The only respite I had was when I put on the molar mascot costume and danced for the children, who howled with laughter. I hoped it was educational and fun for them; for me, it was liberating and cathartic.

But even those brief moments of joy vanished one afternoon when my best friend, my dance partner in the toothbrush mascot costume, slipped while doing his best to show the kids how to clean a molar and accidentally hit my lips with his head. As I hid behind a tree blotting my bleeding lips dry and missing home, a young mother in the village with her baby slung on her back handed me something. We didn't have a common language, but I could tell it was her way of comforting me with food—which always worked. It was eggs grilled in a bamboo stalk half. The eggs were dotted with small pieces of *hom chu*, a local allium (*Allium chinense*) used in the everyday cooking of the area. She pointed at my lips, mimed "soft enough to eat," and walked away. It was a gesture of kindness that has stuck with me all these years. That was also the first time I had eggs prepared that way.

This recipe, called *khai pam*, is the more urban version of the same dish, but it's still considered a traditional northern Thai specialty. It is cooked over charcoal in a "boat" made of banana leaves, and it turns out creamy, smoky, and comforting. (See page 85 for tips on purchasing and handling banana leaves.) I call for Chinese chives, a variety with tender, flat, somewhat pungent blades, but you can swap in green onions. And feel free to replace the shrimp with small pieces of cooked crabmeat, diced leftover grilled chicken, or other cooked meat—or use both to make things more interesting. Don't get carried away with the add-ins, however. The eggs should get the spotlight here.

SERVES 4

>> CONTINUED

Prepare a medium-high fire (400° to 450°F) in a charcoal grill using the two-zone method (see page 11).

Meanwhile, make four "boats": Lay a banana leaf rectangle on a work surface and top it with a second rectangle, lining them up perfectly. Using both hands, grab the two corners on one short end of the stacked rectangles and fold them both toward the middle, then secure the fold with a wooden toothpick. Do the same with the other short end. You should have something that looks like a canoe. Repeat with the remaining banana leaves to create four boats.

In a large bowl, combine the eggs, water, shrimp, chives, chiles, and salt and mix well. Divide the mixture evenly among the four boats.

When the coals are covered with white ash and the grate is hot, carefully place the boats on the grill on the hold side. Cover and cook with the vents half-opened until the egg mixture barely jiggles in the center when a boat is shaken, 20 to 30 minutes. If you like, at this point you can capsize the boats onto the hot side of the grill to brown the tops.

Transfer the boats to a platter and garnish with more chives and chiles. Serve warm.

GRILLED KABOCHA SQUASH
with Coconut Custard Sauce

This is one of my favorite desserts to make on the grill in the early fall—that transition period between summer and autumn—when the market is flooded with different types of pumpkin and winter squash. It's just a tad too cold to grill outside, yet you do it anyway, knowing you'll walk back into the house with a most satisfying warm dessert in hand.

SERVES 4

Put the egg and the egg yolks into a heatproof bowl, then set the bowl near the stove. In a 1-quart saucepan (preferably with a pour spout), combine the coconut milk, sugar, salt, and pandan leaves (if using vanilla extract, add it later) and heat over medium heat, stirring frequently, until the mixture bubbles gently around the edge of the pan. Immediately remove from the heat and discard the pandan leaves.

Now, temper the eggs so they don't curdle: Using one hand, pour ½ to ¾ cup of the hot mixture into the eggs while using the other hand to whisk the eggs until homogenous. Scrape the egg–coconut milk mixture back into the saucepan, return the pan to medium heat, and heat, whisking constantly, until the mixture thickens and registers 170°F on an instant-read thermometer. Remove from the heat (if you are using vanilla extract, whisk it in now) and strain through a fine-mesh sieve into a heatproof bowl. Cover with plastic wrap, pressing it directly against the surface of the custard. Keep warm.

Prepare a medium-high fire (400° to 450°F) in a charcoal grill using the two-zone method (see page 11).

Meanwhile, cut the squash lengthwise into wedges that measure 2 inches at the widest part. Trim off the stem end and scrape off the seeds and fiber. There's no need to peel the pieces unless you want to (I like kabocha squash peel, but your mileage may vary).

When the coals are covered with white ash and the grate is hot, put the kabocha wedges on the hold side of the grill. Cover and cook with the vents half-opened, turning them once, until fork-tender but still very firm, about 20 minutes (this depends largely on the thickness of the squash, which varies quite greatly and won't be seen until you cut it). Move the squash to the hot side of the grill and cook with the lid off until lightly charred on all sides, about 2 minutes.

Transfer the squash wedges to a platter. Check the consistency of the custard. If it has thickened beyond the point of being pourable, whisk in a little more coconut milk or warm water to thin it. Pour the sauce over the grilled squash. Serve warm.

1 large egg

4 egg yolks

2 cups unsweetened full-fat coconut milk, plus more as needed

¾ cup packed grated palm sugar or granulated coconut sugar, or ½ cup packed light brown sugar

⅛ teaspoon salt

2 pandan leaves, each tied into a knot, or 1 teaspoon vanilla extract

One small kabocha squash, weighing about 1¼ pounds

NOTE

Grown throughout Southeast Asia, pandan (or pandanus) leaves are prized for their fragrant aroma. They're available fresh and frozen at most Southeast Asian stores with a large produce section. If you have purchased frozen leaves, hold them under hot running water to thaw before using.

SMOKED EGGS

with Spicy Garlic-Shallot Relish

You can't talk about the many different ways people all over the world cook eggs without turning into Forrest Gump's friend Benjamin Buford "Bubba" Blue, who rattled off ways to prepare shrimp. In Southeast Asia alone, there are countless ways to cook this simple ingredient, including burying whole eggs in mud or sand on a hot day—a practice done long ago in the rural areas of northeastern Thailand. In cities in Laos, Thailand, and Cambodia, you'll also see street hawkers selling *khai ping*, eggs—still in their shells—grilled and smoked over low coals.

My great-grandfather's cook, Aunt Sali, used to cook eggs by burying them whole in wood embers just when the fire in her clay grill was almost spent. At that stage, the coals are hot enough to cook and impart its smoky flavor to the eggs, yet not so hot as to cause the fragile shells to burst. She would snack on those smoky eggs in the afternoon, cutting them in half and topping them with a quick relish made from pantry ingredients.

This recipe is a more convenient way of smoking eggs: with a smoker and hickory wood for the fuel.

SERVES 4 AS AN APPETIZER

In an 8-quart stockpot, bring the water to a boil over high heat and stir in the salt. Working quickly, use a ladle to gently drop the eggs, one by one, into the boiling water. Boil for 7 minutes (use a timer; you need to be exact), stirring five or six times during the first minute to center the yolks. Immediately drain off the water and refill the pot with cold water. When the water becomes warm, drain it off and then repeat the process twice. After draining off the second cold bath, the eggs should be cool enough to handle. Peel them (they should peel easily) and dry them with a clean kitchen towel.

Using hickory wood, set a smoker to 225°F. When the smoker reaches the target temperature and the smoke runs clear, oil the grate and place the eggs directly on it, spacing them about 1 inch apart. Close the lid and smoke until the eggs turn bronze, 20 to 25 minutes. Transfer them to a plate to cool.

Meanwhile, make the relish. In a bowl, stir together the shallots, garlic, chiles, lime juice, fish sauce, and sugar. Taste and adjust the seasoning with more fish sauce if needed. The relish should be sour and salty, with a faint trace of sweet. Be careful not to add too much, though, or the relish will be liquidy.

Halve the eggs lengthwise and arrange them, cut side up, on a platter. Spoon the relish evenly over the eggs and serve immediately.

4 quarts water

¼ cup salt

12 large chicken or duck eggs, at room temperature

½ cup thinly sliced shallots

¼ cup thinly sliced garlic

6 to 8 fresh bird's eye chiles, thinly sliced

¼ cup fresh lime juice

1 tablespoon fish sauce

½ teaspoon granulated sugar

SMOKED COCONUT CAKE

1½ cups granulated sugar

2 large eggs, at room temperature

2 large egg whites, at room temperature

½ teaspoon jasmine extract, or 1 teaspoon vanilla extract

½ teaspoon salt

1 cup all-purpose flour

3½ cups shredded unsweetened dried coconut

This may very well be the cake that put me on the path not only of writing this book but also of writing about anything related to food. One of my earliest memories is of an old lady approaching me, smiling, and offering me a piece of cake that had the most amazing fragrance my little nose had ever encountered. It was only later that I learned the woman was my maternal great-grandmother and that piece of cake was this smoked coconut cake. My great-grandmother died when I was very little, and I have no recollection of anything about her other than that day and that piece of cake with its astonishing scent. I'd like to think that maybe my curiosity about food began that day.

My great-grandmother made all of her baked goods in a large cylindrical clay stove built in the late 1800s. It had roughly the same dimensions as a thirty-gallon steel drum, with a chamber at the bottom where the charcoal went and a perforated clay grate set about one-third of the way down from the top where she put the food. A metal plate acted as a lid as well as the place where she put glowing coals to brown the surface of the food underneath it. My great-grandmother made her fragrant coconut cake—dense and chewy inside and crisp on the top—in this oven, using a combination of coconut husks, dried corn husks, bagasse, and local wood for fuel.

Not equipped with the same tool, I make her *sali krop* with my pellet grill/smoker, using cherrywood for fuel.

⟨──────────────────────────────⟨ **MAKES SIXTEEN 2-INCH SQUARES**

Set a smoker to 350°F. Spray an 8-inch square baking pan with cooking spray. Line the pan with parchment paper.

In a stand mixer or in a bowl with a handheld mixer, beat together the sugar, eggs, and egg whites on high speed until pale and thick enough to form a ribbon when you lift the beater and let the mixture fall back on itself. Using a rubber spatula, fold in the jasmine extract, salt, and flour, being careful not to deflate the eggs. Stir in the coconut flakes just until evenly distributed (the batter will be thick). Transfer the batter to the prepared pan and smooth the surface with a moistened rubber spatula.

When the smoker reaches the target temperature and the smoke runs clear, put the pan directly on the grate, close the lid, and bake until a toothpick or the tip of a knife inserted into the center comes out clean, 50 to 60 minutes.

Remove from the smoker and let cool on a wire rack to room temperature. Cut into 2-inch squares and serve. The bars can kept in an airtight container at room temperature for up to 3 days.

GRILLED BANANAS
with Coconut–Palm Sugar Syrup

In Thailand, this ubiquitous street snack, known as *kluai thap*, calls for slowly grilling peeled *nam wa* bananas over low coals until the exteriors firm up and form a shell protecting the flesh inside, which has become soft and sweet. The grilled bananas are then flattened with a wooden paddle. The shell breaks in the process, allowing the soft flesh inside to ooze out just enough for it to drink up the sweet coconut–palm sugar syrup you shower over it. This is similar to *pisang epe* in Indonesia among others (Southeast Asians love their grilled bananas).

I honestly can't think of a better banana for this recipe than *nam wa*, but you can use plantains with great results. Make sure your bananas are neither too green nor too ripe. The peels should be mostly yellow with some green left near the stems, and with no dark spots or bruises.

1 cup packed grated palm sugar or granulated coconut sugar, or ¾ cup packed light brown sugar

1½ cups coconut milk

½ teaspoon salt

1 pandan leaf (see Note, page 195), tied into a knot (optional)

¼ cup unsalted butter

8 medium half-ripe *nam wa* bananas, or 4 plantains (see headnote and Note)

SERVES 4

In a 2-quart saucepan, combine the sugar, coconut milk, salt, and pandan leaf, if using, and bring to a boil over medium-high heat, whisking often to dissolve the sugar. Lower the heat and simmer, uncovered, until the mixture is reduced by one-third, about 8 to 10 minutes. Stir in the butter, remove from the heat, discard the leaf, and set aside.

Prepare a medium fire (350° to 375°F) in a charcoal grill using the two-zone method (see page 11).

Keep the bananas (or plantains, if using) in their peel until you're ready to grill them in order to prevent discoloration. When the coals are covered with white ash and the grate is hot, peel the bananas and place them on the hold side of the grill near the center where it meets the hot side (if using plantains, peel them with a knife and halve them crosswise). With the lid off, grill the bananas without turning them until the side that touches the grate turns matte, is completely dry to the touch, and is very lightly charred, about 15 minutes. Continue to cook the bananas, rolling them with tongs as needed for even cooking, until they look dry and lightly charred on all sides. Each banana should have formed a slightly hard shell, which can be tested by squeezing it gently with tongs. The whole process should take 30 to 35 minutes.

Remove the bananas from the grill. While they are still hot, place one in the center of a thin wooden cutting board. Place another thin wooden cutting board on top of the banana and press down to flatten it. Don't go overboard and press too hard; you want the banana to be about one-third of its original thickness and no flatter than that. Place the flattened banana on a serving plate. Repeat the process with the remaining bananas.

Drizzle the prepared syrup over the pressed bananas. Serve immediately.

NOTE

Nam wa bananas are only 4 to 5 inches long and fatter than Cavendish bananas, the type usually stocked in US markets. You can find the *nam wa* variety at large Asian grocery stores, and they are often labeled as "Thai bananas."

RECOMMENDED READING LIST

For more in-depth information on the equipment, techniques, and science behind grilling and smoking, as well as general cooking, I recommend the following books.

Franklin, A., and J. Mackay. *Franklin Barbecue: A Meat-Smoking Manifesto*. San Francisco: Ten Speed Press, 2015.

Goldwyn, Meathead. *Meathead: The Science of Great Barbecue and Grilling*. Boston: A Rux Martin Book, Houghton Mifflin Harcourt, 2016.

Lampe, Ray. *Ray Lampe's Big Green Egg Cookbook: Grill, Smoke, Bake & Roast*. Kansas City: Andrews McMeel Publishing, 2016.

López-Alt, J. Kenji. *The Food Lab: Better Home Cooking Through Science*. New York: W. W. Norton, 2015.

McGee, Harold. *On Food and Cooking: The Science and Lore of the Kitchen*. New York: Scribner, 2004.

Mixon, Myron. *BBQ&A with Myron Mixon: Everything You Ever Wanted to Know About Barbecue*. New York: Abrams, 2019.

Stone, Tuffy. *Cool Smoke: The Art of Great Barbecue*. New York: St. Martin's Griffin, 2018.

Wiviott, Gary. *Low and Slow: Master the Art of Barbecue in 5 Easy Lessons*. Philadelphia: Running Press, 2009.

ACKNOWLEDGMENTS

Big thanks to the team at Ten Speed Press, Dervla Kelly, Betsy Stromberg, Lisa Bieser, Erin Skeen Dominguez, Kim Keller, Dan Myers, Deborah Kops, Sharon Silva, and Kathy Brock for shepherding this project to completion with their expertise and insights.

Thanks to the talented David Loftus for the photography and to Pip Spence for her styling genius and loveliness as a person.

Thanks to Harold McGee, Meathead Goldwyn, Pat Tanumihardja, Tracey Paska, and Ige Ramos for lending their expertise to the project and for taking the time to answer my questions. Thanks to Ray Lampe and Max Good for their guidance on grilling tools and equipment.

Thanks to my friends Jem, Jess, and Lisa for their friendship and hospitality, and for sharing their recipes and wisdom with me so generously.

Thanks to my readers whose continued support makes me want to be a better writer every day.

Most of all thanks to my family and friends in both Bangkok and Chicago whose love has sustained me.

INDEX

G

galangal, 102

garlic
Crispy Garlic, 64
Garlic Rice, 79
Spicy Garlic-Shallot Relish, 197

Ghee-Smoked Chicken and Rice
with Spicy Mint Sauce, 73–74

Ginger, Pickled, 98

gloves, heat-resistant, 7

Goldwyn, Meathead, 11, 66

Grape Salad, Spicy, Caveman-Style Reverse-
Seared Rib-Eye Steaks with, 162–65

Green Curry Beef Skewers with
Fried Basil Oil, 176–78

grilling
equipment and tools for, 4, 6–7
fuels for, 7, 11
methods for, 11, 14

H

halibut
Grilled Fish with Fresh Herbs in
Banana Leaf Packets, 25

hati babi bungkus, 136

hau nuong mo hanh, 35

Hay-Smoked Chicken, 68–70

"Heavenly" Racks of Lamb, 161

herbs
Grilled Fish with Fresh Herbs in Banana
Leaf Packets, 25
Herb-Filled Grilled Fish with Spicy
Tamarind Dipping Sauce, 20–23

hibachi grills, 6

Honey-Roasted Duck with Pickled Ginger
and Chile-Soy-Vinegar Sauce, 97–98

I

ikan pari bakar sambal, 32

inasal na manok, 78

J

Jerky, Grilled Pork Sausage, 143–44

jin som, 169

K

kai op fang, 68

kai yang, 56

kai yang bang, 88

kai yang kolae, 94

kamado grills, 6

kanap pa, 25

kapi, 32

kecap manis, 81

kettle grills, 4

ketupat, 90

khai pam, 192

khai ping, 197

khao niao, 56

kluai thap, 201

kroeung, 169

kung mae nam phao, 45

kung siap, 30

L

Lamb, "Heavenly" Racks of, 161

lechon liempo, 112

lemongrass
Grilled Stuffed Lemongrass, 179–80
Lemongrass Grilled Chicken with
Crispy Garlic and Spicy Bamboo
Shoot Salad, 62–66

limes
Cedar-Plank Salmon Salad Bites, 19
Smoked Shrimp with Chile-Lime Dipping
Sauce, 30

Lobster Tails, Grilled, with Fish Sauce–Chile
Butter, 45–46

lontong, 90

López-Alt, J. Kenji, 162

M

mackerel
Grilled Mackerel with Three-Flavored
Sauce, 38
Smoked Fish with Rice, Fried Egg, and
Tomatoes, 42–44

Madura Chicken Satay with Easy Rice
Cakes, 90–92